GOD PRINTS

Bible FUNSTUFF

PAPER CAPERS

The LORD is my rock, my fortress and my deliverer

Jesus is risen!

WRITTEN BY
Lois Keffer

Dedication
To Christy and Nathan who light our lives with joy.

Bible FUNstuff Paper Capers
Copyright © Lois Keffer

Published by Cook Communications Ministries

Scripture quotations, unless otherwise noted, are from

THE HOLY BIBLE, NEW INTERNATIONAL VERSION (NIV)
Copyright © 1973, 1978, 1984 by International Bible Society.
Used by permission of Zondervan Publishing House. All rights reserved.

Edited by: Dawn Renee Weary
Art Direction: Mike Riester
Cover Design: Granite Design
Interior Design: iDesignEtc.
Illustrators: Lois Keffer, Christy Randall

Printed in the United States

First printing, 2002
1 2 3 4 5 6 7 8 9 10   06 05 04 03 02 01

ISBN 0781438365

CONTENTS

Introduction

Ever since I can remember, sheets of paper have been my wings for flights of imagination. And now, as a teacher, paper is one of my most valuable tools in the classroom—not to mention one of the most readily available. Just think what kids can do with a sheet of paper!

Fold it.
Snip it.
Mold it.
Rip it.
Roll it.
Dip it.
Pull it.
Clip it.
Sculpt it.
Nip it.
Shred it.
Grip it.
Fly it.
Strip it.
Stamp it.
Flip it.

A blank sheet of paper is an open-ended invitation to self-expression and learning. The creative possibilities are endless.

Do you know what else is wonderful about paper? Color! Passionate purple, obnoxious orange, lemon pucker-me yellow and really rich ruby red. Color triggers all kinds of wonderful things in our minds. It evokes emotion and tickles the imagination. It's irresistible.

Paper Capers is your ticket to hours of Bible fun with kids at church or at home. Because you can just photocopy and go, you'll always have a treasure trove of learning ideas at your fingertips.

I know you and your kids will have a delightful time exploring God's Word with the ideas packed in these pages. Work your way straight through the book, pick and choose projects to enhance a lesson or meet a child's need, or simply fill a few minutes with meaningful fun.

As you create all kinds of nifty paper creations, you'll be introducing kids to the living God who reveals himself through his Word. What could be better than that?

Paper doesn't last forever, but God's touch does. Thanks for letting me be your partner in ministry to God's kids.

God rules!

Lois Keffer

SUPPLIES

Stocking up for your adventure into *Paper Capers* will give you an hour or two of great fun. Raid your old boxes of art supplies. Become a paper monger! Skip two café lattes and go on a little paper buying spree at your local office supply store. (If you're like me you won't dare go into an arts and crafts store or you'll come out at least twenty dollars poorer!) Keep in mind what will go easily into your church photocopy machine.

Keep a couple of rolls or folded packages of bright foil and holographic wrapping papers on hand. Kids think it's a great treat to get to use these special papers from time to time.

SUPPLIES

Now here's an idea that will make you pop a wheelie: pack your *Paper Capers* supplies into a rolling suitcase. All the nifty little pockets and storage compartments make great tuck-it-away spots for glue sticks, scissors, colored pencils, markers and your favorite stickers. Zip it up and you're ready to roll!

Before the Beginning

Get List

* photocopies of p. 9
* scissors
* glue sticks
* colored pencils
* newspaper

"In the beginning...God!" Help kids stretch their minds to embrace the "forever-and-everness" of God with stretchy words and aged parchment that stands in stark contrast to today's news.

Bible Verses

In the beginning God... **(Genesis 1:1)**.

Before the mountains were born or you brought forth the earth and the world, from everlasting to everlasting you are God **(Psalm 90:2)**.

Go For It!

1. Photocopy p. 9 onto parchment-colored paper.

2. Cut out the background and the two strips with the word "everlasting" on them. Accordion-fold the strips on the dotted lines.

3. Demonstrate how to glue the beginning and ending square of each folded strip to the squares marked on the background. The stretchy words will spring across the page!

4. Lay sections of newspaper out on the table. Have kids trace around the background piece and cut out several layers of newspaper.

5. Fan the newspaper pieces behind the background piece to form a frame and glue it in place. Mount the finished project on a blank sheet of parchment.

BEFORE THE MOUNTAINS WERE BORN OR YOU BROUGHT FORTH THE EARTH AND THE WORLD,

FROM ☐ TO ☐

☐ YOU ARE GOD ☐ PSALM 90:2

| E | V | E | R | L | A | S | T | I | N | G |

| E | V | E | R | L | A | S | T | I | N | G |

The World Is Born

Get List

* photocopies of p. 11
* scissors
* glue sticks
* star stickers
* gold and silver pens

Watch your kids' eyes glow with delight as they transform a flat sheet of paper into an eight-page booklet complete with pop-ups that highlight the incredible power of God in creation.

Bible Verse

In the beginning God created the heavens and the earth. Now the earth was formless and empty, darkness was over the surface of the deep, and the Spirit of God was hovering over the waters **(Genesis 1:1-2)**.

Go For it!

1. Photocopy p. 11 onto dark blue paper.

2. Fold the paper in half horizontally and cut on the heavy line between the dots.

3. Open the paper, then fold it along the dotted line that runs through the mountain and stars. Cut the heavy line at the top of the mountain between the dots. Unfold.

4. Fold on the dotted line that runs through the word "God" and the two frames. Cut the heavy lines on the word "God" between the dots. Unfold.

5. Lay the paper flat. Let kids add star stickers above "created the heavens." Use metallic pens to outline the word "God."

6. Fold the paper in half the long way. Push the side panels toward the center until they meet and form a booklet. Pull the mountains and the word "God" forward to make them pop up. Glue the undersides around the backgrounds of the pop-ups to hold the pages together.

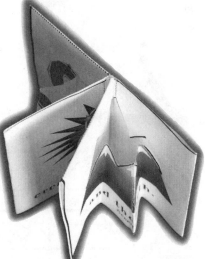

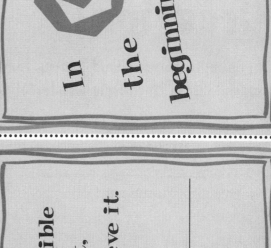

In the beginning

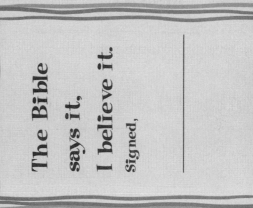

The Bible says it, I believe it.
Signed,
_____

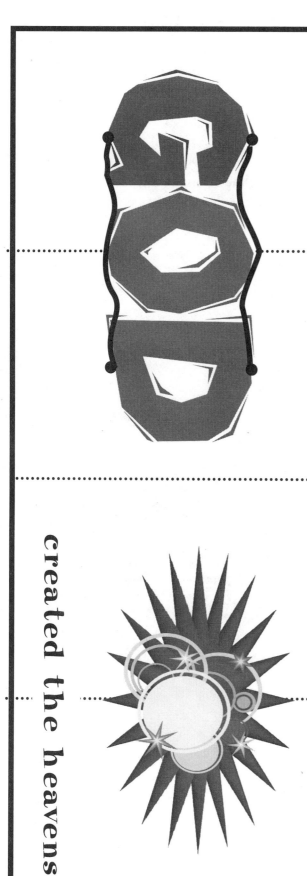

created the heavens

and the earth.
Genesis 1:1

Five-Star Creation!

Get List

* photocopies of p. 13
* scissors
* glue sticks
* markers, gel pens

This simple personalized pop-up reminds kids that they're made in the image of our matchless, infinitely wonderful Creator.

Bible Verse

So God created man in his own image, in the image of God he created him; male and female he created them **(Genesis 1:27)**.

Go For It!

1. Photocopy p. 13 onto bright yellow paper.

2. Cut the card out on the solid lines. Fold it in half the long way so the pictures show. Fold the pop-up section back and forth on the dotted lines, and then lay the card flat.

3. Fold the card in half horizontally so the pop-up section faces you. As you fold the card closed, fold the pop-up section toward you. *Note:* The card will be folded at the bottom and open at the top.

4. Have kids write their names in fun letters across the pop-up section, then personalize the rest of the card with information about themselves.

5. When they've finished, glue the edges of the card together, taking care to leave the pop-up section free.

Made in his very own image, the Creator himself brings you

THE ONE THE ONLY...

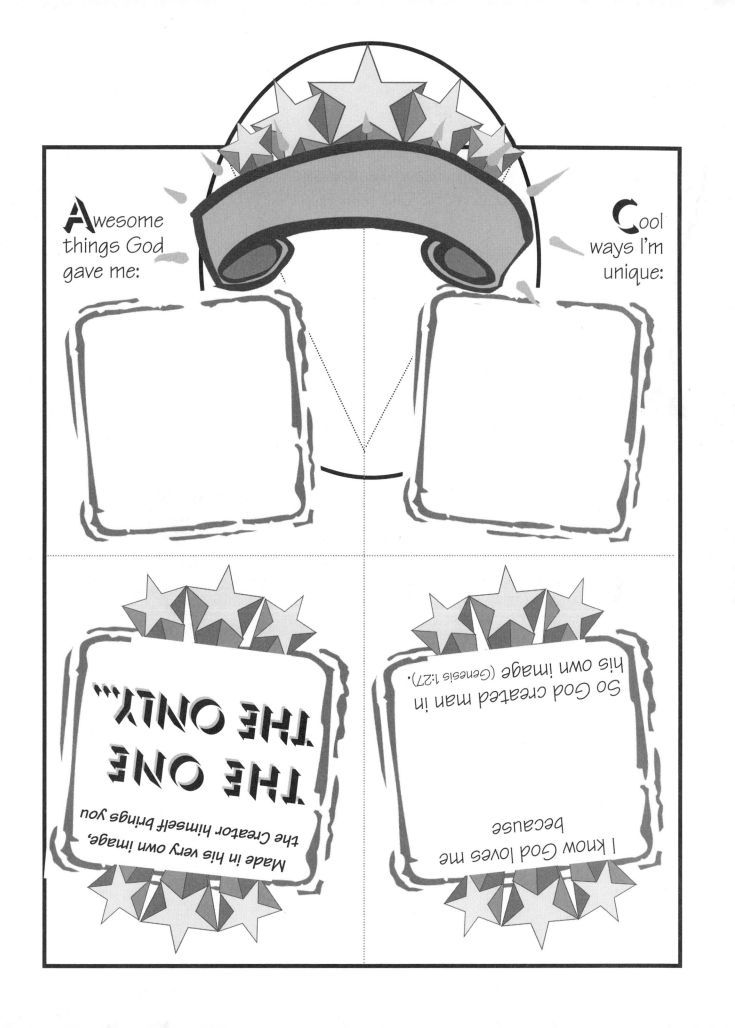

Awesome things God gave me:

Cool ways I'm unique:

"THE ONE THE ONLY..."

Made in his very own image, the Creator himself brings you

So God created man in his own image (Genesis 1:27).

I know God loves me because

Ark Hanger

Floating serenely under the rainbow, this clever ark with its door that opens will remind kids to keep their hope in the Lord, no matter what the circumstances!

Get List

* photocopies of p. 15
* scissors
* markers
* hole punch
* ribbon

Bible Verses

I have set my rainbow in the clouds, and it will be the sign of the covenant between me and the earth **(Genesis 9:13)**.

Be joyful in hope **(Romans 12:12)**.

Go For It!

1. Photocopy p. 15 onto sturdy white paper.

2. Fold the paper in half the long way on the dotted lines and crease well.

3. While still folded, cut out the figure. Carefully cut away the area between the ark and the rainbow. Then cut on the solid lines around the door on one side. *Note:* You may want to have more skilled kids help their friends with this step.

4. Open the paper and color it.

5. Fold back the tabs beneath the doors and glue them together. The door will pop open!

6. Carefully punch a hole in the center of the rainbow. Tie a bright ribbon through the hole to hang your ark!

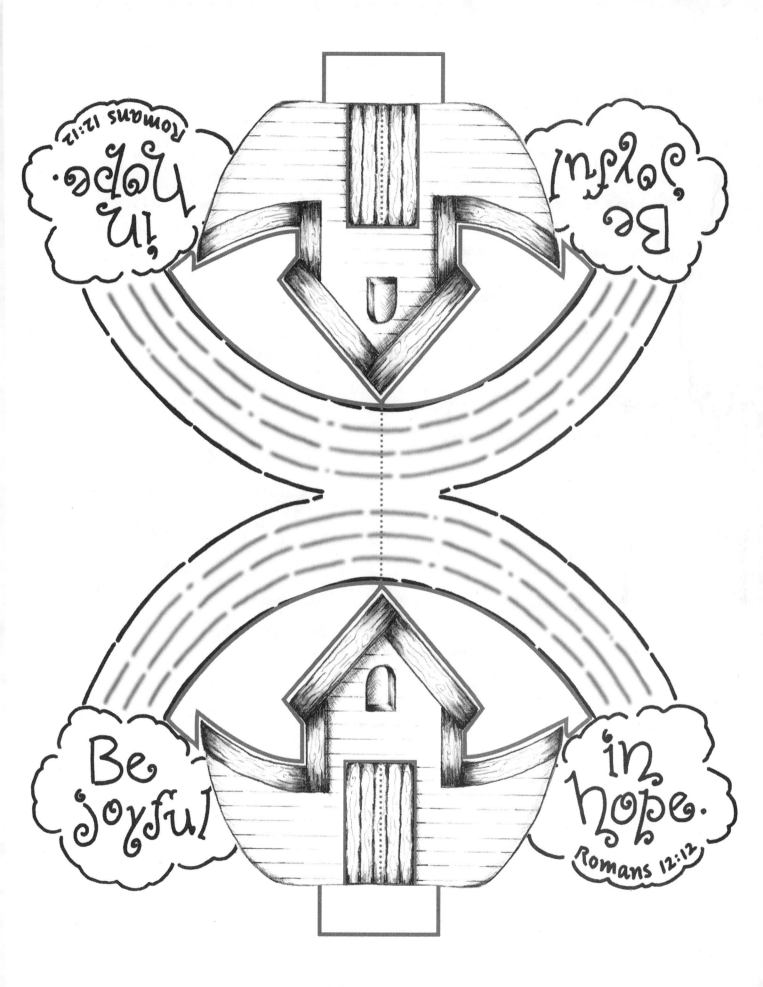

Starry, Starry Promise

Get List

* photocopies of p. 17
* scissors
* pencils with eraser tips
* stick pins

Abraham's head must have spun when God promised that his descendants would be as countless as the stars in the sky. This spinner details God's promise. Set it spinning, and the starts seem to multiply!

Bible Verse

I will make your descendants as numerous as the stars in the sky and will give them all these lands, and through your offspring all nations on earth will be blessed **(Genesis 26:4)**.

Go For It!

1. Photocopy p. 17 onto copier paper.

2. Cut out the circle and fold it on all the dotted lines.

3. Recrease all the folds so that one is a mountain fold, the next is a valley fold, and so forth around the circle.

4. Push a stickpin through the dot in the center and into the eraser end of a pencil.

5. Show the kids how to spin the circle and make the stars seem to multiply! Talk about how God kept his promises to Abraham.

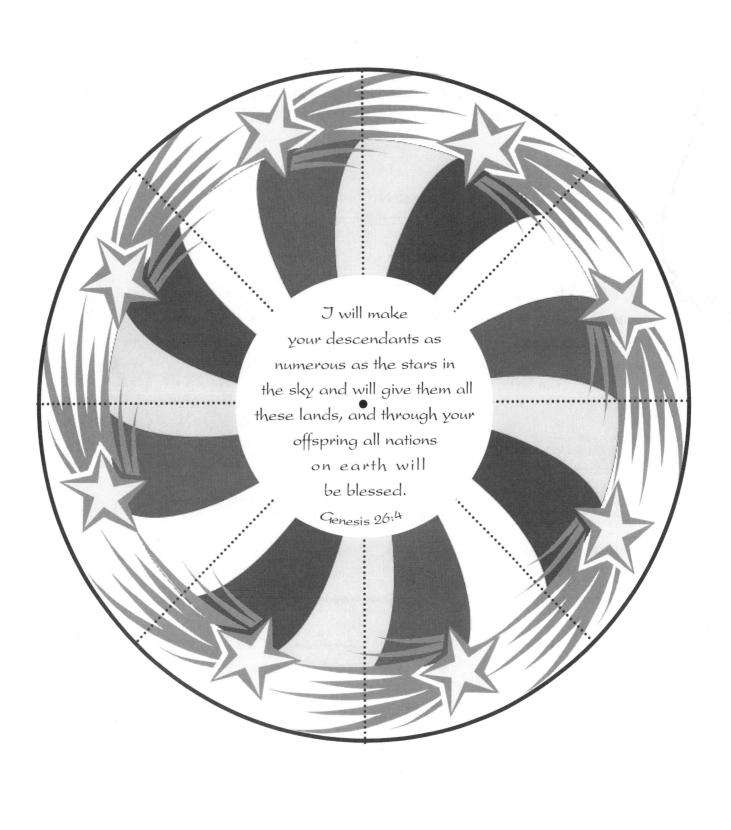

I will make
your descendants as
numerous as the stars in
the sky and will give them all
these lands, and through your
offspring all nations
on earth will
be blessed.

Genesis 26:4

What a Stew!

Get List

* photocopies of p. 19
* scissors
* markers, gel pens

Isaac's family wasn't the only one to get in a stew instead of getting along. This folded stew pot will help kids think about what to do to make peace when family relationships go to pieces!

Bible Verse

But Esau ran to meet Jacob and embraced him; he threw his arms around his neck and kissed him. And they wept **(Genesis 33:4)**.

Go For It!

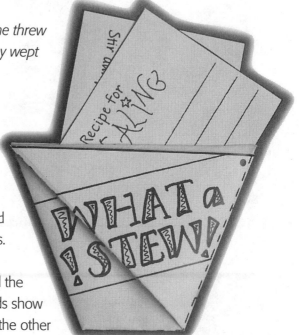

1. Photocopy p. 19 onto copier paper.

2. Cut apart the square recipe cards on the heavy lines. Talk about the story of Jacob and Esau, and have kids finish the recipes with their own words.

3. Cut the stew pot square on the heavy lines. Fold the square diagonally on the dotted line so the words show on the outside. Fold one corner to circle A. Fold the other corner to circle B.

4. Fold the top triangles down on the dotted lines and tuck in the points between the flap pieces.

5. Pull the "stew pot" open.

6. Decorate the stew pot with markers. Tuck the recipe cards inside.

WHAT a STEW!

? !

WHAT to DO? is

fold down and tuck

fold in

fold in

fold down and tuck

B

A

Recipe for
DISAGREEMENTS

Mix a handful of _____

With a dash of _____

Stir daily.

Recipe for
HEALING

Stir plenty of _____

With a dash of _____

Mix daily with _____

Joseph's Red Rocket Coaster Ride

Get List

* photocopies of p. 21
* scissors
* tape
* craft knife
* red holographic ribbon

What's more fun than a roller coaster? Just about anything if the roller coaster happens to be your life! Use this terrific coaster ride to help kids understand that God is with them through all life's ups and downs.

Bible Verse

The warden paid no attention to anything under Joseph's care, because the Lord was with Joseph and gave him success in whatever he did **(Genesis 39:23)**.

Go For It!

1. Photocopy p. 21 onto sturdy paper.

2. Cut out the base and the roller coaster strips on the solid lines.

3. Fold the strips on the dotted lines and tape them to the matching sections of the base to create the hills and valleys of a roller coaster. The strips will overlap at Box 4. Tape the coaster strips so that the words show except for the bottom section that folds under.

4. *Note: eliminate this step with younger, less-skilled students.* Have an adult helper use a craft knife to cut the slits marked on the roller coaster strips. Be sure to cut through all the layers. Let kids weave strips of red ribbon through the roller coaster.

5. As they pull the ribbon to make the roller coaster fly through its course, remind them that God will be faithful to them through all the ups and downs of their lives, just as he was faithful to Joseph.

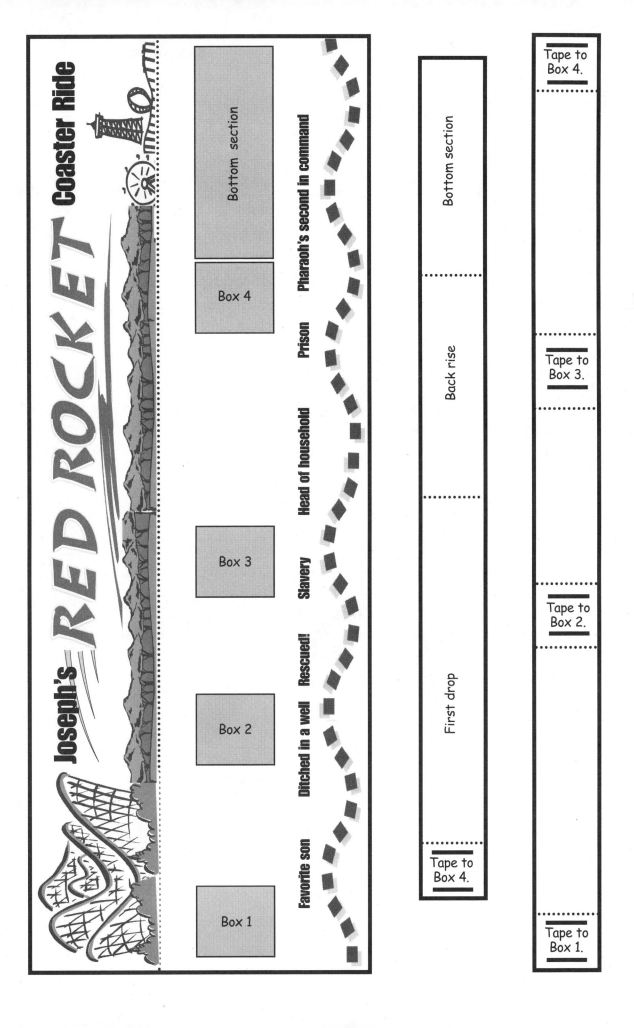

March Through the Sea!

Get List

* photocopies of p. 23
* scissors
* glue stick
* blue glitter glue

Optional
* blow dryer
* fruit-chew bears

When the Israelites found themselves in the most desperate circumstances, what did God say? Don't move a muscle—just trust in my power to deliver you. These curling walls of water celebrate God' great power to deliver us no matter what the situation.

Bible Verses

Moses answered the people, "Do not be afraid. Stand firm and you will see the deliverance the Lord will bring you today. The Egyptians you see today you will never see again. The Lord will fight for you; you need only to be still" **(Exodus 14:13-14)**.

Go For It!

1. Make photocopies of p. 23 on dark blue paper.

2. Cut the sections apart on the dark lines. Fold in the dotted lines. Roll the edges of the waves around smooth pencils so they curve out, creating walls of water.

3. Glue the smaller section inside the larger one. Edge the waves with blue glitter glue. Let a helper dry the glitter glue with a blow dryer.

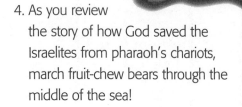

4. As you review the story of how God saved the Israelites from pharaoh's chariots, march fruit-chew bears through the middle of the sea!

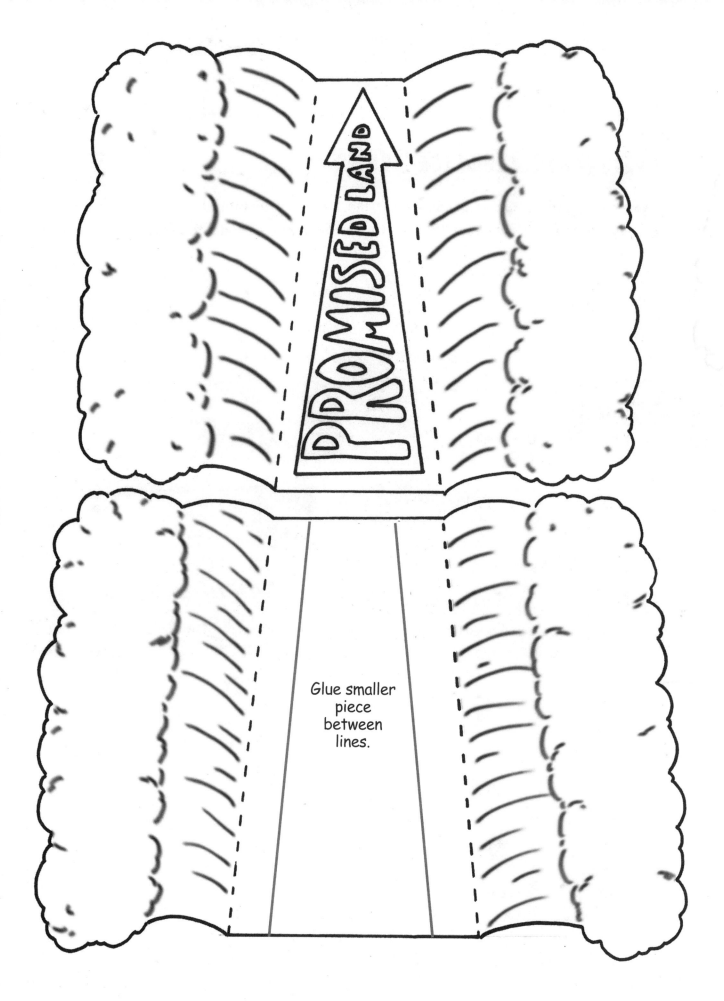

PROMISED LAND

Glue smaller
piece
between
lines.

Can o' Commandments

If you could open a can of goodness for the kids in your ministry, what would you cook up for them? How about the Ten Commandments—God's foundation for right relationships. Mmm, good!

Bible Verse

And God spoke all these words: "I am the LORD your God, who brought you out of Egypt, out of the land of slavery. You shall have no other gods before me" **(Exodus 20:1-3)**.

Go For It!

1. Photocopy p. 25. Use a craft knife to cut the slit on the left side of the can.

2. Cut out the figure on the solid lines. Fold back on the dotted lines.

3. Close the can by slipping the tab into the slit.

4. Talk with kids about the fact that God loves us so much that he gave us the Ten Commandments so our lives would be "Mmm-good"!

1. YOU SHALL HAVE NO OTHER GODS BEFORE ME.

2. YOU SHALL NOT MAKE FOR YOURSELF AN IDOL.

3. YOU SHALL NOT MISUSE THE NAME OF THE LORD YOUR GOD.

4. REMEMBER THE SABBATH DAY BY KEEPING IT HOLY.

Can o'
Commandments

Mmm...good for you!

Goodness from God's Word
GOD'S TOP TEN

5. HONOR YOUR FATHER AND YOUR MOTHER, SO THAT YOU MAY LIVE LONG IN THE LAND.

6. YOU SHALL NOT MURDER.

7. YOU SHALL NOT COMMIT ADULTERY.

8. YOU SHALL NOT STEAL.

9. YOU SHALL NOT GIVE FALSE TESTIMONY AGAINST YOUR NEIGHBOR.

10. YOU SHALL NOT COVET.

Memories of Moses

Get List

* photocopies of p. 27
* scissors
* glue sticks
* markers

With a few simple snips and folds, unfold the thrilling life of Moses layer by layer!

Bible Verse

Since then, no prophet has risen in Israel like Moses, whom the Lord knew face to face
(Deuteronomy 34:10).

Go For It!

1. Photocopy p. 27.

2. Cut around the figure, then cut it apart on the heavy line.

3. Turn the pieces so the blank side faces you. Place the larger piece on top of the smaller one. Glue the centers together.

4. Fold the Ten Commandments page forward so the text faces you and glue it to the center piece.

5. Fold the burning bush forward, then the basket in the river, then the title page. As you review the events of Moses' life, talk about how he knew God in a very special way.

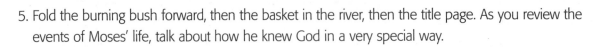

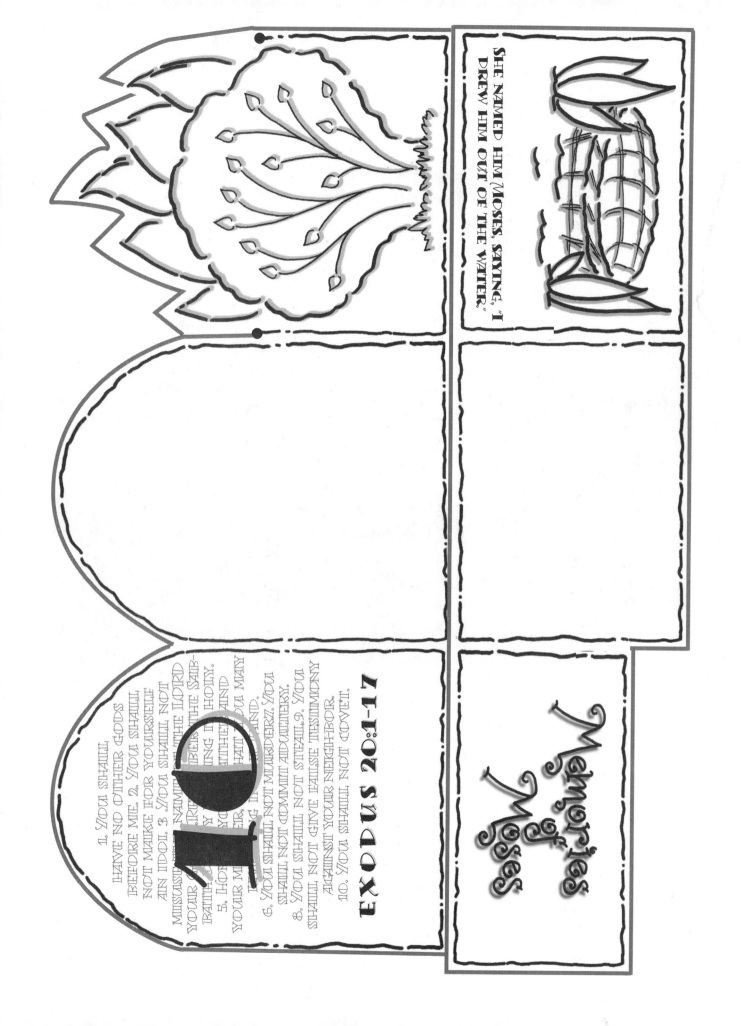

SHE NAMED HIM MOSES, SAYING, "I DREW HIM OUT OF THE WATER."

EXODUS 20:1-17

1. YOU SHALL HAVE NO OTHER GODS BEFORE ME. 2. YOU SHALL NOT MAKE FOR YOURSELF AN IDOL. 3. YOU SHALL NOT MISUSE THE NAME OF THE LORD YOUR GOD. 4. REMEMBER THE SAB-BATH DAY BY KEEPING IT HOLY. 5. HONOR YOUR FATHER AND YOUR MOTHER, THAT YOU MAY LIVE LONG IN THE LAND. 6. YOU SHALL NOT MURDER. 7. YOU SHALL NOT COMMIT ADULTERY. 8. YOU SHALL NOT STEAL. 9. YOU SHALL NOT GIVE FALSE TESTIMONY AGAINST YOUR NEIGHBOR. 10. YOU SHALL NOT COVET.

Memories of Moses

The Shema

This simple-to-fold piece gives kids a glittering stand-up reminder of the foundational faith statement of Judaism and Christianity. Over the centuries, God's people have traditionally begun the day with this statement of faith.

Get List

* photocopies of p. 29
* markers
* glitter glue

Optional
* hair dryer

Bible Verse

Hear, O Israel: The LORD our God, the LORD is one. Love the LORD your God with all your heart and with all your soul and with all your strength **(Deuteronomy 6:4-5)**.

Go For It!

1. Photocopy p. 29 on copier paper.

2. Cut out the piece on the exterior lines.

3. Fold the top and bottom back on the dotted lines.

4. Fold the sides back on the inner dotted lines.

5. Fold the sides forward on the inside edge of the leaf pattern.

6. Let kids decorate the leaf pattern and letters with markers and glitter glue. Have a helper dry the glitter glue with a blow dryer.

Hear, O Israel:
The LORD our God,
    the LORD is one.
Love the LORD your God
    with all your heart
and with all your soul
and with all your strength.

Hold It!

God honored craftspeople with the important jobs of creating the tabernacle and the tools the priests used in worship. These simple containers the kids create can hold their craft supplies and encourage their creative urges!

Get List

* photocopies of p. 31 on card stock
* half sheets of construction paper
* scissors
* markers
* glue sticks

Optional
* yogurt cups

Bible Verse

I have given skill to all the craftsmen to make everything I have commanded you **(Exodus 31:6)**.

Go For It!

1. Photocopy p. 31 on card stock.

2. Fold the paper on the center line and cut out the circles. Unfold.

3. Make valley folds on the two dotted lines near the edges of the paper.

4. Make mountain folds on the dashed lines near the circles. Voila! You have a stand.

5. Let kids use fancy bubble letters to add their names to the blank paint splat.

6. Glue the bottom edges to a half sheet of construction paper.

7. Slip a yogurt cup into each circle to form a handy holder for craft supplies. Brainstorm with kids ways they can use their artistic and creative abilities to honor God.

I have given skill to all the craftsmen
to make everything I have commanded you.
Exodus 31:6

Choose the Lord!

A house glowing with God's love—that's what kids will come away with as this project challenges them to choose God's way.

Get List

* photocopies of p. 33
* scissors
* glue sticks
* markers

Bible Verse

Choose for yourselves this day whom you will serve…but as for me and my household, we will serve the Lord **(Joshua 24:15)**.

Go For It!

1. Photocopy p. 33 on copier paper.

2. Cut out the two house shapes.

3. On the back house—the one with no illustrations—use yellow markers to create a "glow" around the words. Set the back piece aside.

4. Fold the front piece of the house down the center so the illustrations show. Carefully clip the top and bottom of the door and middle window. Unfold the house, then clip the center lines of the door and window. Fold the doors and widows open on the dotted lines. Fold the next set of dotted lines, and then cut the tops and bottoms of the two side windows. Clip the center of these windows and fold the windows open.

5. Glue the front house piece to the back piece so the words show through the windows.

6. Talk with the kids about what it means to accept Joshua's challenge. Have them add their signatures and the date inside the door. Encourage them to have their family members sign it as well!

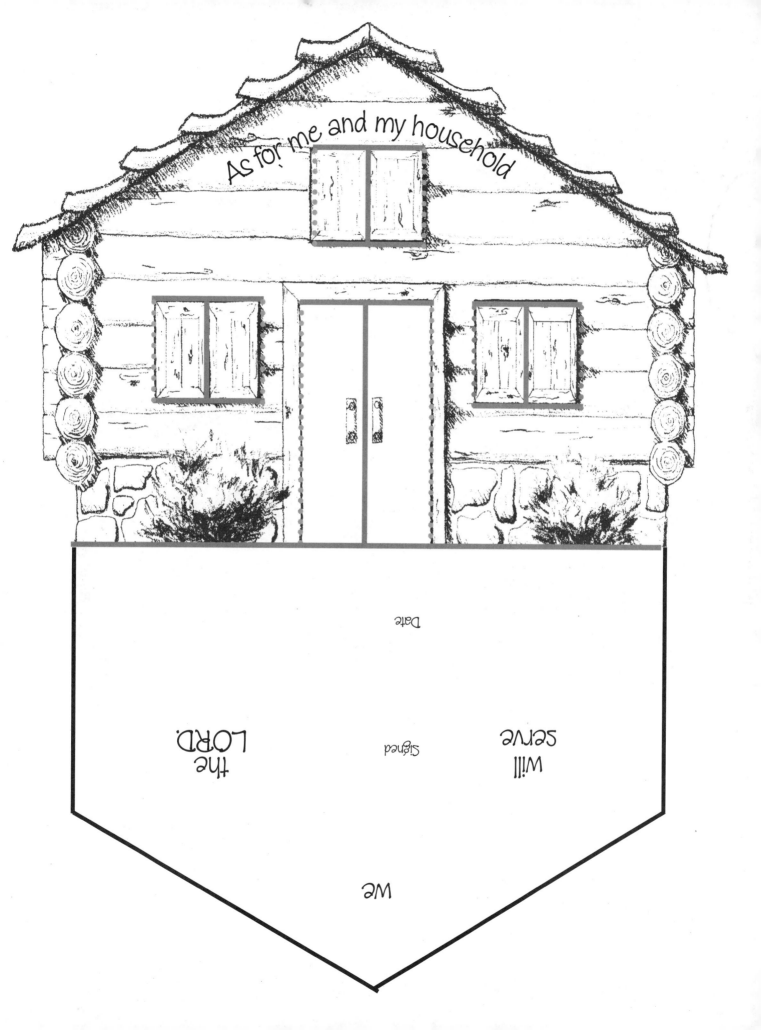

Steppin' Out Around Jericho

Get List

* photocopies of p. 35
* scissors
* glue sticks

This model of the falling walls of Jericho will teach kids that when we step out in obedience, God takes care of the rest.

Bible Verse

The seventh time around, when the priests sounded the trumpet blast, Joshua commanded the people, "Shout! For the Lord has given you the city!" **(Joshua 6:16)**.

Go For It!

1. Photocopy p. 35 onto copier paper.

2. Cut out the two pieces on the solid lines. Fold the background piece forward so the pictures don't show. Unfold.

3. Fold back all the dotted lines on the city wall piece. Curve the side pieces back to form towers and glue the last section to the back of the wall.

4. Match the top and bottom tabs of the city wall to the rectangles on the background and glue them.

5. When you flatten the background, the walls of Jericho fall down! Talk with kids about how God's people "stepped out" in obedience and followed God's unusual battle plan.

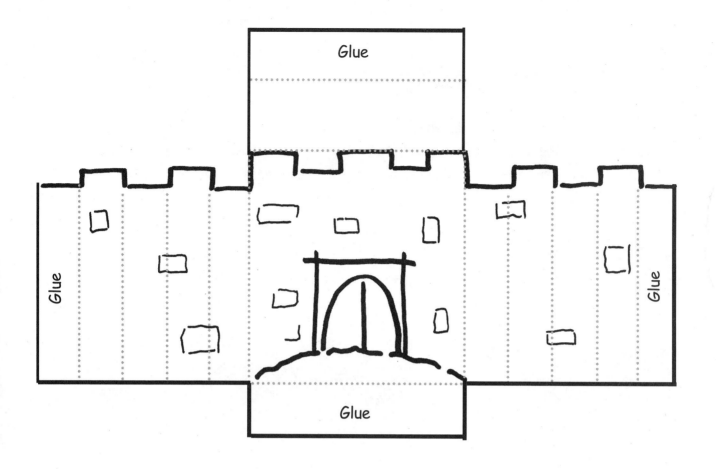

Glue

Glue

Glue

Glue

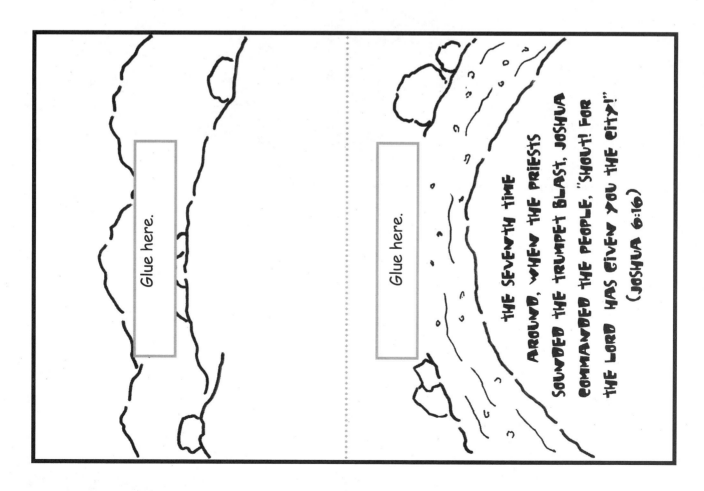

Glue here.

Glue here.

THE SEVENTH TIME
AROUND, WHEN THE PRIESTS
SOUNDED THE TRUMPET BLAST, JOSHUA
COMMANDED THE PEOPLE, "SHOUT! FOR
THE LORD HAS GIVEN YOU THE CITY!"
(JOSHUA 6:16)

Forever Love

Get List

* photocopies of p. 37
* scissors
* glue sticks

There's no greater gift you can give your kids than knowing what God is like. This quick-to-make pop-up in the round will teach kids that he is God above all gods who keeps his covenant of love to a thousand generations.

Bible Verse

Know therefore that the LORD your God is God; he is the faithful God, keeping his covenant of love to a thousand generations of those who love him and keep his commands **(Deuteronomy 7:9)**.

Go For It!

1. Photocopy p. 37 onto copier paper.

2. Cut out the figure. Follow the interior lines to cut away the middle spaces below the hearts.

3. Fold back where the hearts connect. Fold back the tab at the edge. Fold the rectangles forward on the dotted lines.

4. Glue the tab to the back of the first heart to form a pop-up in the round.

5. Talk with kids about all the ways God is amazing!

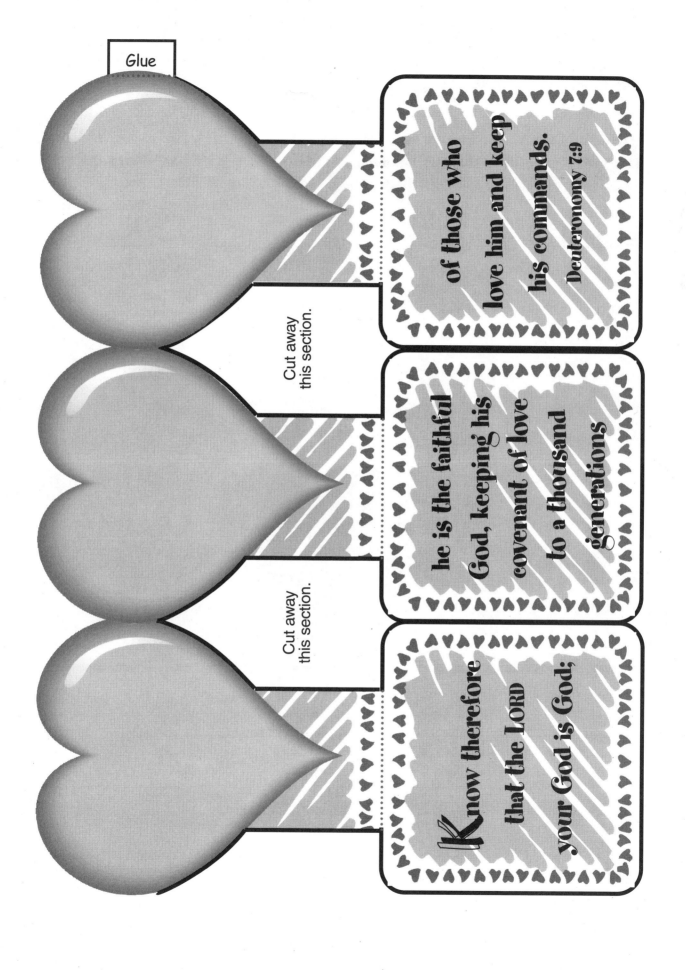

Glue

Cut away this section.

Cut away this section.

of those who love him and keep his commands. Deuteronomy 7:9

he is the faithful God, keeping his covenant of love to a thousand generations

Know therefore that the LORD your God is God;

Stars of My Life

Get List

* photocopies of p. 39
* scissors
* gel pens

David and Jonathan treasured each other as friends. This quick-to-make autograph foldout book will help your kids celebrate the important friendships in their lives.

Bible Verse

Jonathan said to David, "Go in peace, for we have sworn friendship with each other in the name of the LORD" (**1 Samuel 20:42**).

Go For It!

1. Photocopy p. 39 onto brightly colored paper.

2. Cut out the two sections of three boxes each. Make one long strip by gluing the tab at the end of the first section to the back of the second section.

3. Accordion-fold the pages to form a book.

4. Review the story of David and Jonathan with your kids. Talk about what characteristics the kids appreciate in their friends. Then break out the gel pens and have an autograph party!

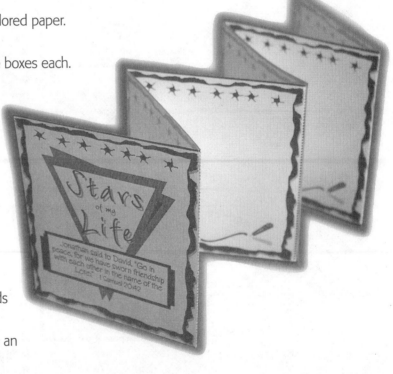

Stars of my Life

Jonathan said to David, "Go in peace, for we have sworn friendship with each other in the name of the LORD." 1 Samuel 20:42

Fortress of Refuge

Get List

* photocopies of p. 41
* scissors
* glue sticks
* markers
* pencils
* toothpicks
* 10" lengths of twine

A 3-D castle with a working drawbridge—what could be cooler than that? As kids create and personalize this castle, they'll learn that God will always be there for them in times of trouble.

Bible Verse

The LORD is my rock, my fortress and my deliverer; my God is my rock, in whom I take refuge (**Psalm 18:2**).

Go For It!

1. Photocopy p. 41 onto copier paper.

2. Cut out the three pieces: the background, the drawbridge with the verse and the castle. Fold the background in half so the pictures don't show, then open it again. Carefully use the tip of a pencil to poke through the two dots.

3. Fold the drawbridge in half so the text shows. Glue a toothpick securely inside the fold. Fold the end tabs forward. Glue both end tabs to the drawbridge space on the background.

4. Fold back the tabs on the castle. Glue them to the spaces marked on the background.

5. *Note: eliminate this step with younger students.* Thread the ends of the twine through the holes in the background. Bring the ends through the door of the castle and tie them around the toothpick at the top of the drawbridge.

6. Have kids draw their last names on the pennant in the foreground. Talk about how God can be a fortress—a safe place to go—when they're troubled.

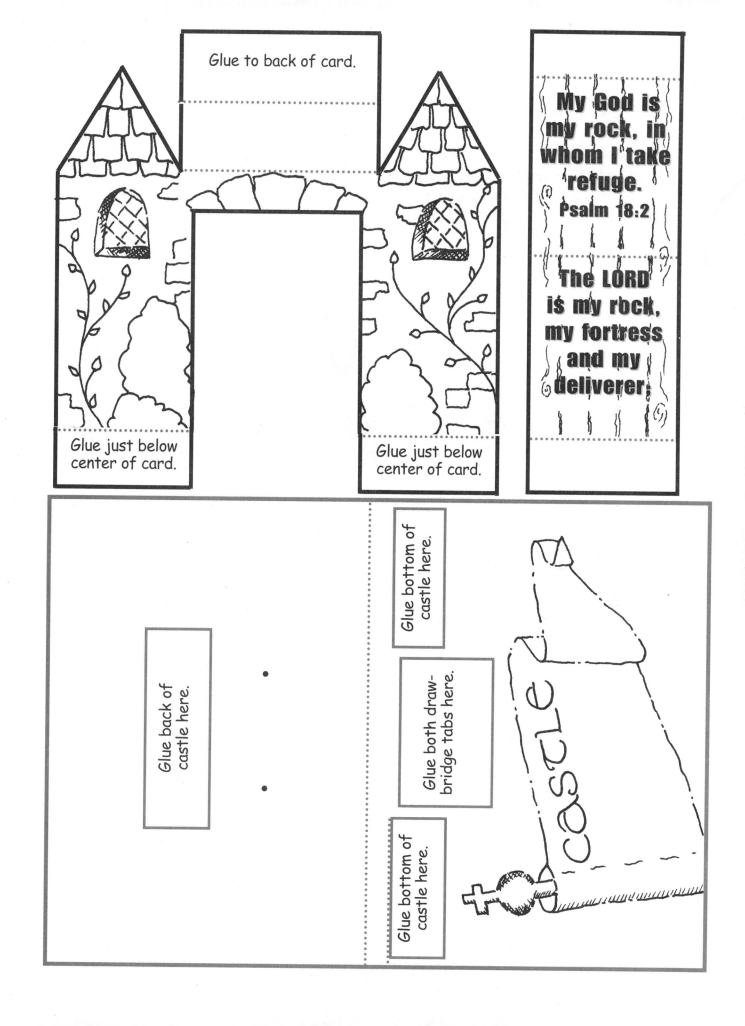

Glue to back of card.

My God is
my rock, in
whom I take
refuge.
Psalm 18:2

The LORD
is my rock,
my fortress
and my
deliverer.

Glue just below
center of card.

Glue just below
center of card.

Glue bottom of
castle here.

Glue back of
castle here.

Glue both draw-
bridge tabs here.

Glue bottom of
castle here.

castle

Heavenly Holder

This handy holder makes a perfect storage spot for notes and other important treasures. And it serves as a ready reminder of how God speaks to us of his glory in the star spangled night sky.

Get List

* photocopies of p. 43
* scissors
* glue sticks
* glitter glue

Optional
* hair dryer

Bible Verse

The heavens declare the glory of God; the skies proclaim the work of his hands **(Psalm 19:1)**.

Go For It!

1. Photocopy p. 43 onto sturdy white paper.

2. Cut out the figure. Fold back the four tabs on the dotted lines.

3. Glue the tabs on each side together to form a container.

4. Add glitter glue sparkles to the stars in the sky. Let a helper dry the glitter glue with a blow dryer.

5. Explain that all of nature speaks to us about the greatness of God the Creator. Invite kids to enjoy some star gazing, and to think of the God who spilled the stars across the sky and set all the worlds spinning in space.

The skies proclaim
the work of his hands.
Psalm 19:1

The heavens declare
the glory of God;

Fold back and glue.

Fold back and glue.

Fold back and glue.

Fold back and glue.

The 23rd Psalm Booklet

Get List

* photocopies of p. 45
* scissors
* glue sticks
* markers, gel pens

Bible Verse

The LORD is my shepherd, I shall not be in want **(Psalm 23:1)**.

Go For It!

1. Photocopy p. 45 onto copier paper.

2. Cut out the two strips. Fold the strip with the title in half with a mountain fold (so the title pages show), then fold the two "sheep pages" to the inside.

3. Fold the strip with the four sheep in half with a valley fold (so the pictures don't show). Make mountain folds on the two dotted lines between the sheep (so the sheep show). Make valley folds on the tabs.

4. Glue the tabs to the middle crease of the title strip. Make sure the sheep with "He makes me lie down…" is closest to the front cover piece. Then cover the tabs with sheep pages from the title strip and glue them in place.

5. Have kids write their names on the back of the booklets and claim the promises in the psalm as their own!

Faith and Flags

This beautiful fusion of scripture and national symbols helps kids understand that true greatness begins in honoring God.

Get List

* photocopies of p. 47
* scissors
* glue sticks

Optional

* shiny red, silver and blue bag stuffing
* Chinet® oval plates

Bible Verse

Blessed is the nation whose God is the LORD **(Psalm 33:12)**.

Go For It!

1. Photocopy p. 47 onto copier paper.

2. Cut out the two pieces.

3. Fold back the four side panels with the flags.

4. Fold forward on the dotted lines near the tips of the flags.

5. Put glue on the blank sides of the end pieces and glue the two halves together.

6. To create a table decoration with patriotic pizzazz, place the figure on a heavy oval paper plate and stuff it with shiny bag stuffing.

7. Talk with kids about how faith in God, and making laws and policies that honor God, makes a nation great.

Blessed is the nation whose God is the LORD.

Psalm 33:12

A Verse with a View

Get List

* photocopies of p. 49
* scissors
* colored pencils

Optional
* glitter glue
* hair dryer

Kids can open and close the cabin shutters on this sunny landscape that's framed by a psalm of joy.

Bible Verse

Where morning dawns and evening fades you call forth songs of joy **(Psalm 65:8)**.

Go For It!

1. Photocopy p. 49 onto copier paper.

2. Cut out the figure on the heavy lines.

3. Make mountain folds on Lines 1 and 4. Make valley folds on Lines 2 and 3. Pull the folds toward the center to make the top and bottom frame.

4. Holding the top and bottom folds together, make mountain folds on Lines 5 and 8. Make valley folds on Line 6 and 7. Pull the folds toward the center to make shutters.

5. As kids highlight the drawings with colored pencils, remind them to turn their thoughts toward God every morning and every evening. If you wish, let them add glitter glue to the rays of the sun.

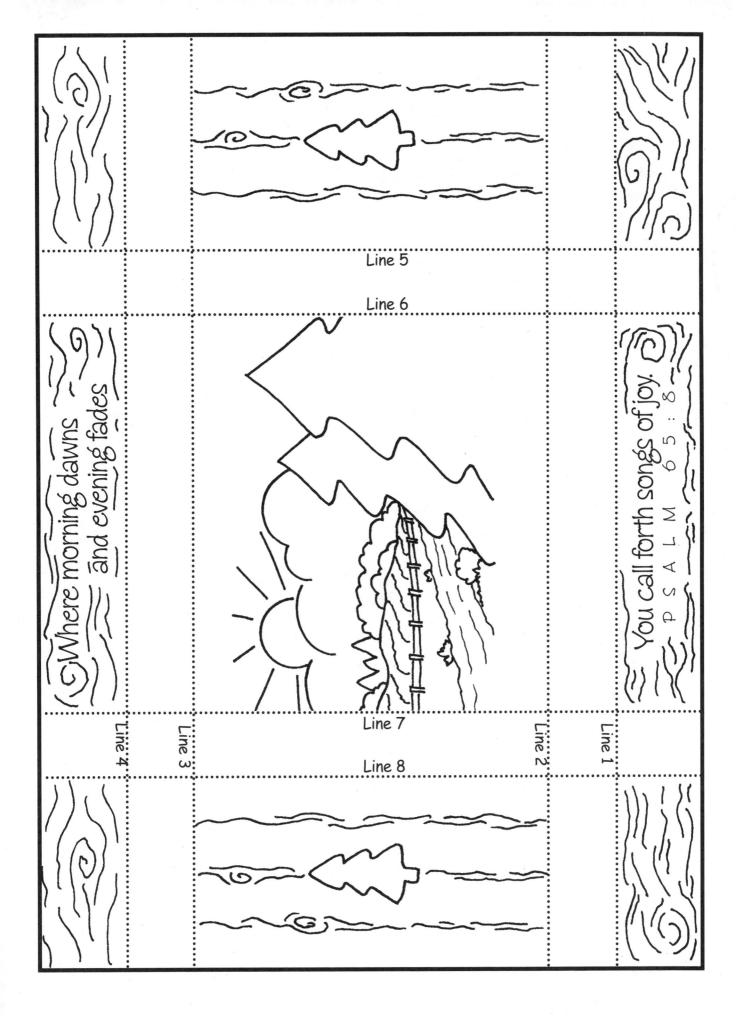

You call forth songs of joy.
P S A L M   6 5 : 8

Where morning dawns
and evening fades

Line 1

Line 2

Line 3

Line 4

Line 5

Line 6

Line 7

Line 8

Bountiful Basket

Celebrate God's blessing at harvest time with a folded basket that overflows with the bounties of candy corn!

Get List

* photocopies of p. 51
* scissors
* glue sticks
* markers or colored pencils

Optional
* ribbon
* hole punch
* candy corn

Bible Verse

You care for the land and water it; you enrich it abundantly. The streams of God are filled with water to provide the people with corn **(Psalm 65:9)**.

Go For It!

1. Photocopy p. 51 onto copier paper.

2. Cut out the basket and the verse tabs on the solid lines. Decorate the basket.

3. Fold the verse tabs back on the dotted lines. Glue the triangular section inside the basket as shown.

4. Glue the basket together with the marked section behind the first section. If you wish, punch holes in opposite sides and tie a ribbon hanger through the holes.

5. As you fill the baskets with candy corn, talk about the blessings God gives us at harvest time.

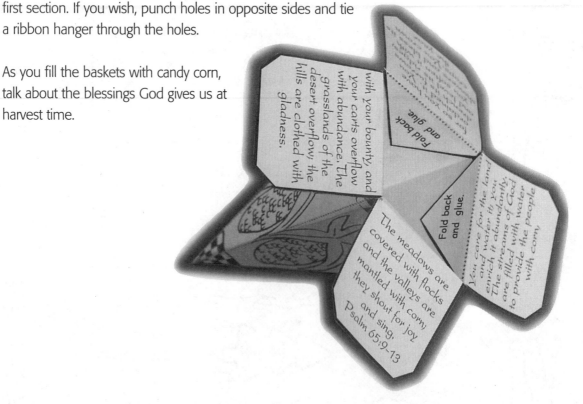

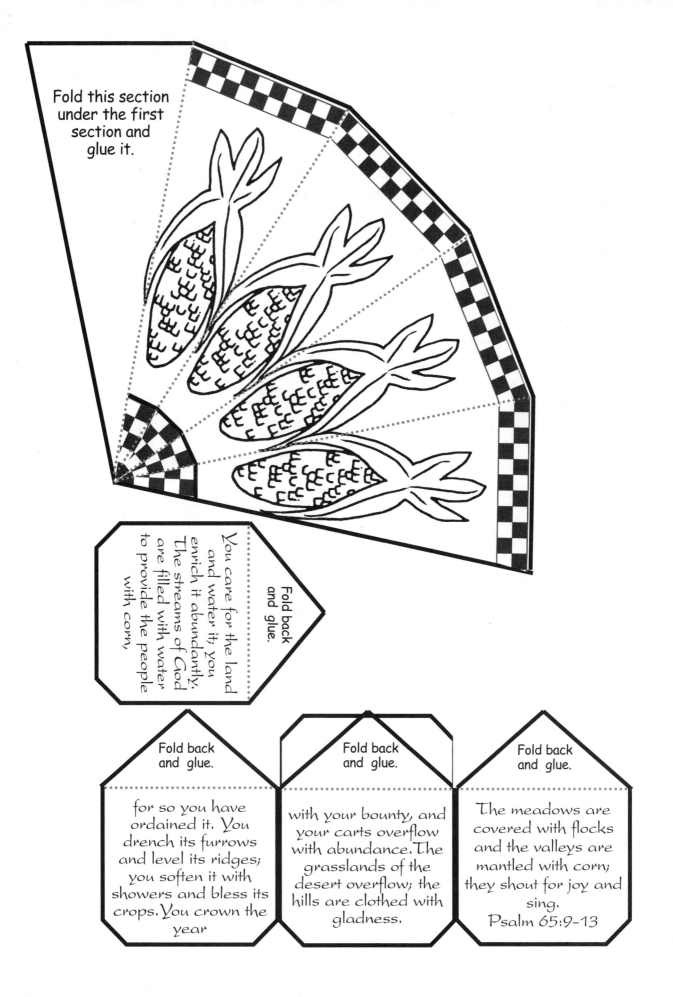

Fold this section under the first section and glue it.

Fold back and glue.

You care for the land and water it; you enrich it abundantly. The streams of God are filled with water to provide the people with corn,

Fold back and glue.

for so you have ordained it. You drench its furrows and level its ridges; you soften it with showers and bless its crops. You crown the year

Fold back and glue.

with your bounty, and your carts overflow with abundance. The grasslands of the desert overflow; the hills are clothed with gladness.

Fold back and glue.

The meadows are covered with flocks and the valleys are mantled with corn; they shout for joy and sing.
Psalm 65:9-13

Guardian Angels

A bent straw and some brads make this guardian angel fly! This positive reminder of God's care can hover just about anywhere—from the car to the bedpost.

Get List

* photocopies of p. 53
* scissors
* brads
* hole punch
* straws

Bible Verse

For he will command his angels concerning you to guard you in all your ways **(Psalm 91:11)**.

Go For It!

1. Photocopy p. 53 onto sturdy paper.

2. Cut out the angel and the wings.

3. Line up the second set of wings behind the angel. Push brads through the dots on the angel and the wings.

4. Bend a straw in the middle. Punch holes one-half inch from each end of the straw and through the dots on the wing tips. Fasten brads through the holes.

5. Move the straw up and down to make the angel fly! Talk with kids about angel stories in the Bible. Ask them when they will remember this promise.

For he will command his angels concerning you to guard you in all your ways.

For he will command
his angels concerning you
to guard you in all your ways.

PSALM 91:11

Mother's Day Card

Get List

* photocopies of p. 55
* scissors
* art supplies and novelties such as tiny buttons or sequins

No one appreciates a homemade card like Mom, and no one deserves it more!

Bible Verse

Give her the reward she has earned, and let her works bring her praise **(Proverbs 31:31)**.

Go For It!

1. Photocopy p. 55 onto sturdy paper. A flecked or natural-looking paper is nice for this project.

2. Cut out the card, trimming carefully around the flowers.

3. Place the card face down. Fold the flower section toward the center, and then fold the front section toward the center.

4. Add a personal message on the center section.

5. Set out your choice of art supplies and novelties such as tiny buttons or sequins. As kids decorate their cards, talk with kids about how good it is to show appreciation to their moms and other caregivers.

You're special
to me because...

HAPPY
Mother's
DAY

to someone special

Wise Up!

What's this friendly owl hiding under his wings? Wisdom from the book of Proverbs that will help set your kids on the right path!

Get List

* photocopies of p. 57
* scissors
* glue sticks
* colored pencils or markers

Bible Verse

Trust in the LORD with all your heart and lean not on your own understanding; in all your ways acknowledge him, and he will make your paths straight **(Proverbs 3:5-6)**.

Go For It!

1. Photocopy p. 57 onto copier paper.

2. Cut out the owl figure. Fold the wings back on the dotted lines so they're hidden behind the owl.

3. Cut the slits on the base. Hook them together to make the figure stand.

4. As kids finish the owl with colored pencils or markers, talk about each of the proverbs. Which do they follow well? Which ones do they need to work at?

In all your ways acknowledge him, and he will make your paths straight. Proverbs 3:5-6

Trust in the LORD with all your heart and lean not on your own understanding;

Father's Day Card

Get List

* photocopies of p. 59
* scissors
* glue sticks
* markers or colored pencils

What does every Dad need for Father's Day? A wild tie, of course! And this one will help kids give a pat on the back and a word of appreciation to the man of the house.

Bible Verse

Parents are the pride of their children **(Proverbs 17:6)**.

Go For It!

1. Photocopy p. 59 onto sturdy paper.

2. Cut out the two ties. Glue the cover tie's knot onto the knot of the second tie.

3. Add some zing with color!

4. As kids write a personal message of appreciation on the bottom tie, encourage them to tell you what they appreciate about their dads.

You're such a

GREAT GUY,

it flips my tie!

HAPPY FATHERS DAY!

Parents are the pride of their children.
Proverbs 17:6

Glue top tie here.

Celebrate Spring!

Get List

* photocopies of p. 61
* scissors
* markers or colored pencils
* glue sticks

In springtime, we're especially focused on God's everyday miracles of new life. God's creation speaks to us in clear, sweet bird song. Celebrate spring with this lovely pop-up.

Bible Verse

Flowers appear on the earth; the season of singing has come, the cooing of doves is heard in our land **(Song of Solomon 2:12)**.

Go For It!

1. Photocopy p. 61 onto sturdy paper.

2. Cut out the background and the bird. Decorate the background with bright colors.

3. Fold the bird in half, and then fold the wings and tail back on the dotted lines.

4. Glue the folded tail pieces to the space marked on the background. The bird will rise from the background as if it's taking flight!

5. As kids enjoy the pop-up action they've created, encourage them to tell you what they like best about spring. Praise the God of creation together!

The winter is past;
The rains are over and gone.

Flowers appear on the earth;
The season of singing has come,
The cooing of doves is heard
in our land. SONG OF SOLOMON 2:11-12

Glue folded tail here.

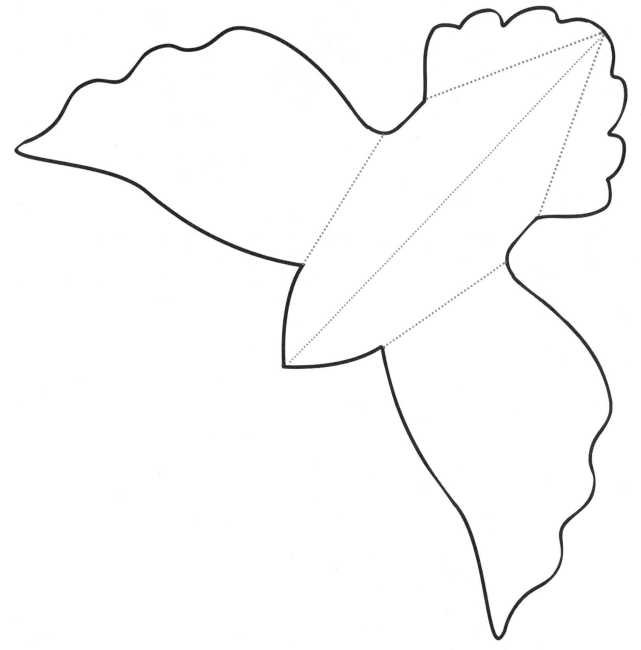

Josiah's Treasure

A hidden treasure moved the heart of the king—
it was the Word of the Lord, which had been lost
in the crumbling temple. Josiah rededicated
himself and his people to following God's Word.
This treasure box will help your kids do the same.

Get List

* photocopies of p. 63
* scissors
* craft knife
* markers
* silver and gold gel pens

Bible Verse

*Then the king called together all the elders
of Judah and Jerusalem. He went up to
the temple of the LORD with…all the
people from the least to the greatest. He
read in their hearing all the words of the
Book of the Covenant, which had been
found in the temple of the LORD* **(2 Kings 23:1-2)**.

Go For It!

1. Photocopy p. 63 onto parchment colored paper.

2. Cut out the box and the Treasure Cards. Decorate them with gold and silver gel pens.

3. Have kids write their names on the Treasure Box, then fold it on the dotted lines to form a box.

4. Have a helper open the slit on the boxes with a craft knife.

5. Help kids write favorite Bible verses on the Treasure Cards, then
drop the cards in the box and close it. As kids write,
talk about Josiah's discovery and recommitment
to God's Word.

Treasure
Card

2 Kings 23:1-2

Treasure
Box

Then the king called together all
the elders of Judah and
Jerusalem. He went up to the
temple of the LORD with…all the
people from the least to
the greatest. He read in their
hearing all the words of the Book
of the Covenant, which had been
found in the temple of the LORD.

Treasure
Card

Clapping Trees!

Get List

* photocopies of p. 65
* scissors
* glue sticks
* tape

The beauty of a single leaf can take your breath away. When fall colors tinge the leaf tips, it really does seem that they clap their hands! Make clapping leaves and help kids give God a hand for the glory of his world.

Bible Verse

You will go out in joy and be led forth in peace; the mountains and hills will burst into song before you, and all the trees of the field will clap their hands **(Isaiah 55:12)**.

Go For It!

1. Photocopy p. 65 onto bright orange, yellow or red paper.

2. Cut out the leaf shapes and the spring. Some kids may want to cut the detailed leaf shape—others can cut loosely around it.

3. Fold the leaves in half on the dotted lines so the patterns show.

4. Fold the springs with a mountain fold in the middle and valley folds on the sides. Glue the middle section together.

5. Place the folded leaf shapes so the middle lines meet. Place the end sections of a spring on the spaces marked on the leaves. Tape the edges of the spring to the leaves.

6. Turn the leaves over and place the second spring on this side.

7. When the glue is thoroughly dried, enjoy clapping the leaves together to honor God who creates each one with detailed delight!

You will go out in joy and be led forth in peace;
the mountains and hills will burst into song before you,
and all the trees of the field will clap their hands
(Isaiah 55:12).

You will go out in joy and be led forth in peace;
the mountains and hills will burst into song before you,
and all the trees of the field will clap their hands
(Isaiah 55:12).

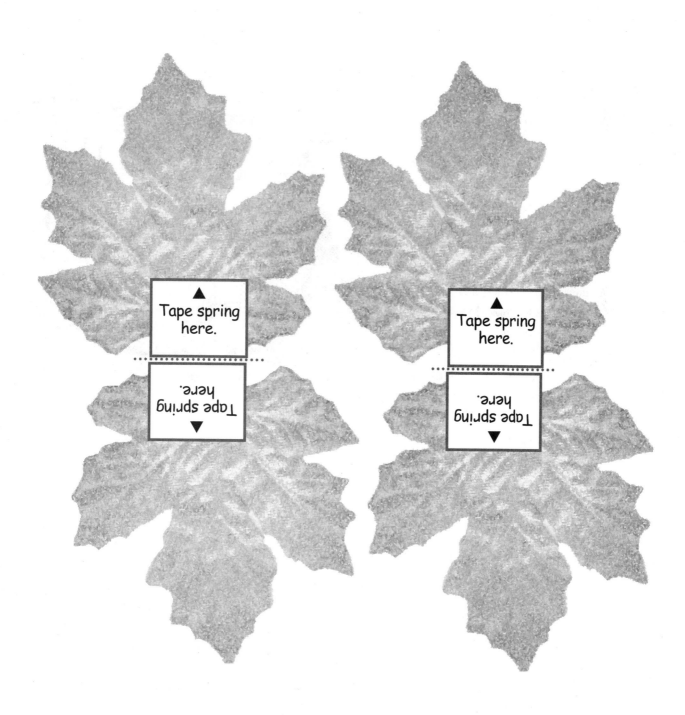

▲
Tape spring
here.

Tape spring
here.
▼

▲
Tape spring
here.

Tape spring
here.
▼

Precious in His Sight

Get List

* photocopies of p. 67
* scissors
* markers, gel pens
* straws or Pixie Stix®

A page about me—now that's a fascinating subject! Kids need to know that no matter how smart or pretty or popular or athletic they are or aren't, they are ever and always precious in God's sight.

Bible Verse

You are precious and honored in my sight (**Isaiah 43:4**).

Go For It!

1. Photocopy p. 67 onto neon colored paper.

2. Cut out the pages on the heavy lines. If you photocopied onto different colors of paper, let kids swap pages so they have more than one color in their books.

3. Fold the pages in half and cut away the indicated areas on the folds. Give kids plenty of time to draw, doodle and decorate their pages.

4. Fold the dotted lines on the spine, and then tuck one page inside the other. Weave a straw through the folded edges to form a spine. Talk about what it means to be precious in the sight of God.

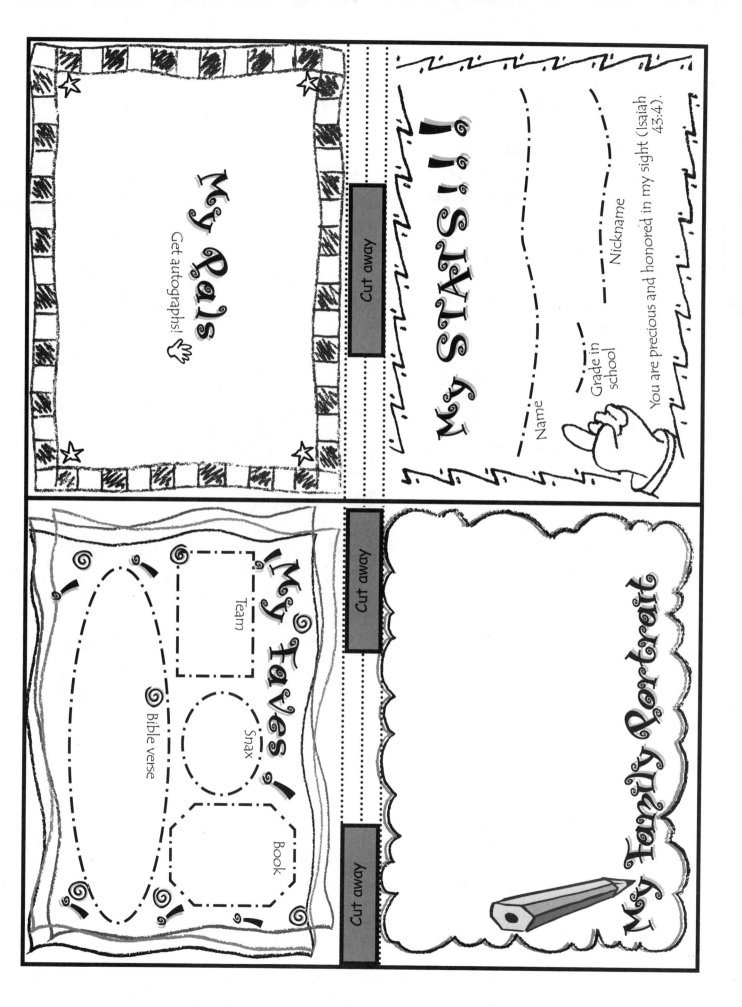

My Pals
Get autographs!

My Stats!!
Name
Nickname
Grade in school
You are precious and honored in my sight (Isaiah 43:4).

Cut away

My Faves!
Team
Bible verse
Snax
Book

Cut away

Cut away

My Family Portrait

Bedtime Comfort

Get List

* photocopies of p. 69
* scissors
* markers, colored pencils

Could there be any more wonderful reminder of God's love than this verse? Your kids will enjoy curling up with the scripture each night at bedtime.

Bible Verse

*The L*ORD* your God is with you, he is mighty to save. He will take great delight in you, he will quiet you with his love, he will rejoice over you with singing* **(Zephaniah 3:17)**.

Go For It!

1. Photocopy p. 69 onto sturdy paper.

2. Cut out the figure on the solid lines. Cut the bedposts as far as the dots.

3. Have the kids write their names in the blank on the headboard and color the quilt and bed.

4. Fold the legs back on the dotted lines.

5. Fold the headboard up; the legs will point down.

6. Fold the footboard down; the second set of legs will point down. Encourage kids to make this their "bedtime verse"!

Windows on Advent

Get List

* photocopies of p. 71
* scissors
* glue sticks
* markers
* glitter glue

Optional

* Christmas stickers

It's always exciting to peek ahead to the wonders of Christmas. The windows on this tree open to reveal wonderful Old Testament prophecies about Jesus.

Bible Verse

Therefore the Lord himself will give you a sign: The virgin will be with child and will give birth to a son, and will call him Immanuel **(Isaiah 7:14)**.

Go For It!

1. Photocopy p. 71 onto green paper.

2. Cut out the tree and the backing piece.

3. One at a time, fold back on the dotted lines on the tree, then cut the heavy lines around three sides of each window.

4. Lay the piece flat, then fold the four window pieces up.

5. Glue the backing piece to the tree so the verses of prophecy about Jesus show through the windows.

6. As kids decorate their trees with markers, shiny stickers and glitter glue, talk about how each one of these Old Testament prophecies about Jesus came true.

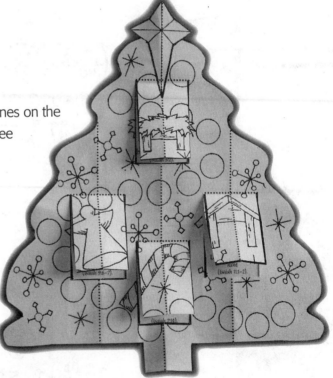

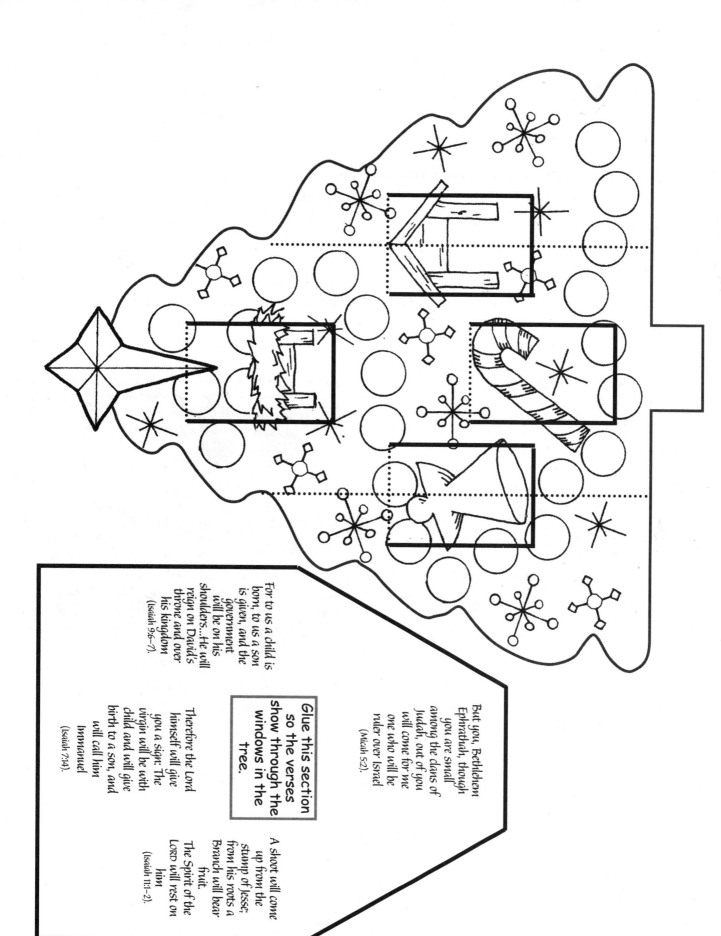

Glue this section
so the verses
show through the
windows in the
tree.

For to us a child is
born, to us a son
is given, and the
government
will be on his
shoulders...He will
reign on David's
throne and over
his kingdom
(Isaiah 9:6–7).

But you, Bethlehem
Ephrathah, though
you are small
among the clans of
Judah, out of you
will come for me
one who will be
ruler over Israel
(Micah 5:2).

Therefore the Lord
himself will give
you a sign: The
virgin will be with
child and will give
birth to a son, and
will call him
Immanuel
(Isaiah 7:14).

A shoot will come
up from the
stump of Jesse;
from his roots a
Branch will bear
fruit.
The Spirit of the
LORD will rest on
him
(Isaiah 11:1–2).

Arise and Shine!

Nothing gives us reason to hope like Jesus coming into the world—and into our lives. Use this glowing star as an invitation for kids to let Jesus light up their lives with his hope!

Get List

* photocopies of p. 73
* scissors
* glue sticks
* markers
* craft knife
* brads

Bible Verse

Arise, shine, for your light has come, and the glory of the LORD rises upon you **(Isaiah 60:1)**.

Go For It!

1. Photocopy p. 73 onto sturdy paper.

2. Cut out the three pieces: the star card, the circle and the stand.

3. Color the spaces of the circle bright yellow and orange. Color the front of the star card deep blue.

4. Let older kids and adult helpers use a craft knife to cut away the triangles that surround the star.

5. Fold the star card in half with the circle in the middle so the glowing colors show through the triangles. Fasten a brad through the center of the front of the card and the circle piece.

6. To make the stand, mountain fold on the center line and valley fold on the outside lines. Glue the stand to the inside of the card as indicated on the stand. Make sure not to glue the circle to the stand.

7. Turn the circle and watch the star glow! Talk about the light and hope that Jesus brings into our lives.

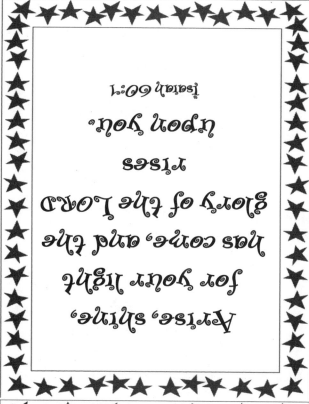

Arise, shine,
for your light
has come, and the
glory of the LORD
rises
upon you.
Isaiah 60:1

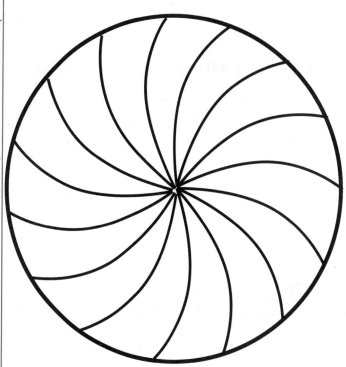

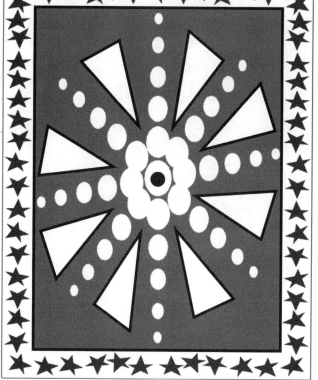

Glue inside back of card.

Glue inside front of card.

Christmas Box

Get List
* photocopies of p. 75
* scissors
* paper punch
* markers
* ribbon

This quick-to-make container can deliver small gifts and treats as it speaks of the greatest gift of all.

Bible Verse

"She will give birth to a son, and you are to give him the name Jesus, because he will save his people from their sins." All this took place to fulfill what the Lord had said through the prophet: "The virgin will be with child and will give birth to a son, and they will call him Immanuel"—which means, "God with us" (**Matthew 1:21-23**).

Go For It!

1. Photocopy p. 75 onto copier paper.

2. Cut out the box and the verse square on the solid lines. Decorate both with markers.

3. Fold all the dotted lines so that the decorations show to form a pyramidal box. Place the verse square inside the bottom of the box.

4. Punch through the dots near the points. Thread ribbon through the holes to tie the box shut. Talk about the great gift God gave the world at Christmas.

"She will give birth to a son, and you are to give him the name Jesus, because he will save his people from their sins." All this took place to fulfill what the Lord had said through the prophet: "The virgin will be with child and will give birth to a son, and they will call him Immanuel"—which means, "God with us" (Matthew 1:21-23).

King in a Manger

Get List

* photocopies of p. 77
* scissors
* glue sticks

This beautiful pop-up card will remind kids of the remarkable birth of the King of kings who came to the world in the humblest possible circumstances.

Bible Verse

This will be a sign to you: You will find a baby wrapped in cloths and lying in a manger **(Luke 2:12)**.

Go For It!

1. Photocopy p. 77 onto copier paper.

2. Cut out the three pieces: the background, the stable and the baby in the manger.

3. Valley fold the background then open. Fold the baby in the manger in half and cut away the shaded areas. Working out from each side of the baby, make a valley fold and then two mountain folds.

4. Glue the bottom of the manger to the space indicated on the background.

5. Fold the stable in half and cut out the middle. Fold the roof of the stable back and forth on the diagonal lines to create a crease. Fold the "legs" of the stable outward on the dotted lines and glue them to the spaces indicated on the background.

6. Kids may want to decorate the pop-up, but it's also beautiful when it's left plain white. Encourage kids to talk about how ordinary and humble Jesus' birth was.

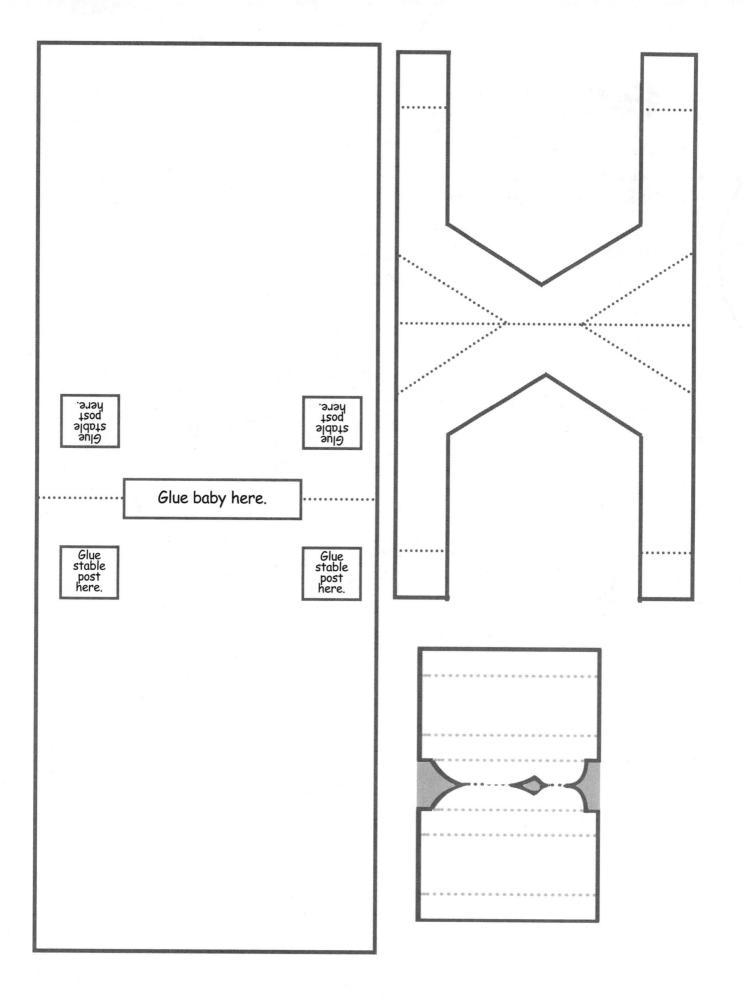

Follow Me!

What does it mean to follow Jesus? This toe-tally cool booklet will help reaffirm their desire to follow Jesus and define their next steps.

Get List

* photocopies of p. 79
* scissors
* glue sticks
* markers

Bible Verse

"Come, follow me," Jesus said **(Matthew 4:19)**.

Go For It!

1. Photocopy p. 79 onto copier paper.

2. Fold the paper in half on the dotted line, then in half again. While it's still folded, cut out the foot shape.

3. Glue the blank sides of the feet together to form a four-page booklet.

4. Talk about what it means to follow Jesus. Help kids thoughtfully fill out each page and share what they've written.

"Come, follow me," Jesus said (Matthew 4:19).

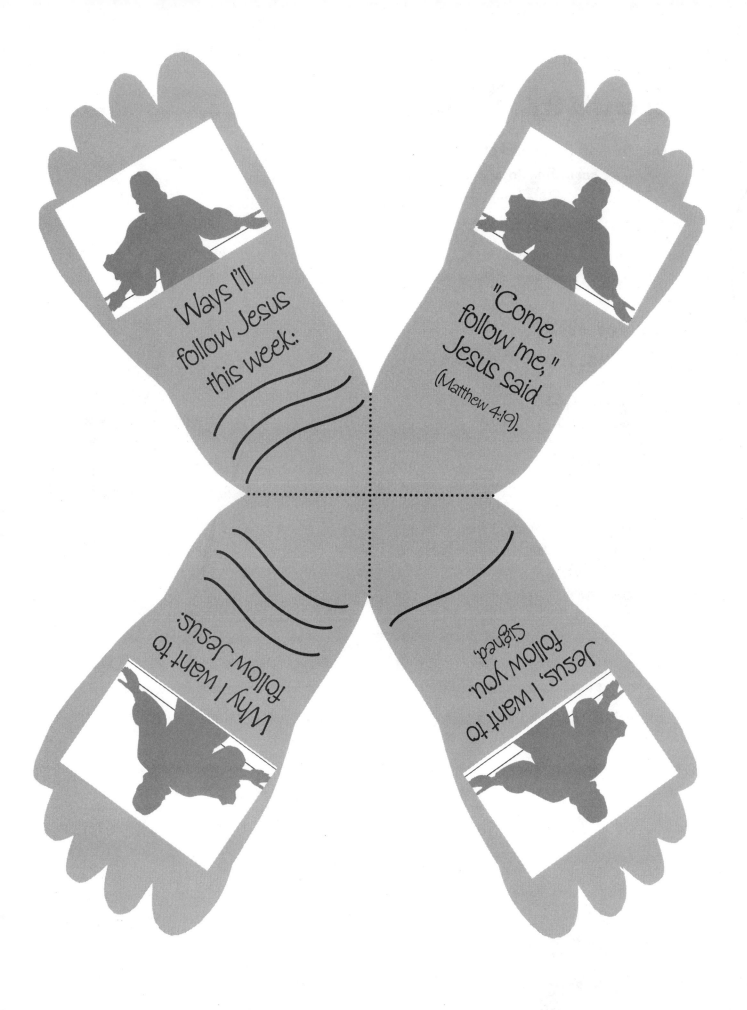

Pocket This!

This fold-up jeans pocket will help kids tune their attitudes according to Jesus' Beattitudes!

Bible Verse

Now when he saw the crowds, he went up on a mountainside and sat down. His disciples came to him, and he began to teach them **(Matthew 5:1-2)**.

Go For It!

1. Photocopy p. 81 onto copier paper.

2. Cut out the pocket on the heavy lines. Carefully cut the slits on the side flaps.

3. Fold all the dotted lines in so the art shows.

4. Fasten the pocket by sliding the slits together. Have kids add their names and decorate the pocket. Explain that trusting Jesus' promise to bless helps us keep a Christlike attitude when times are tough.

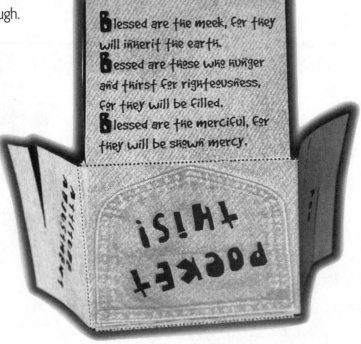

c p a a p p e e r r s

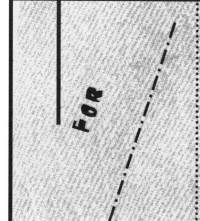

FOR

ATTITUDE ADJUSTMENT

Jesus began to teach them, saying:

Blessed are the poor in spirit, for theirs is the kingdom of heaven.

Blessed are those who mourn, for they will be comforted.

Blessed are the meek, for they will inherit the earth.

Blessed are those who hunger and thirst for righteousness, for they will be filled.

Blessed are the merciful, for they will be shown mercy.

Blessed are the pure in heart, for they will see God.

Blessed are the peacemakers, for they will be called sons of God.

Blessed are those who are persecuted because of righteousness, for theirs is the kingdom of heaven.

Shine On!

It's not easy for kids to do things that make them stand out from the crowd—but that's exactly what Jesus wants them to do. This lighthouse will encourage them to shine for their Lord!

Get List

* photocopies of p. 83
* scissors
* markers
* glue sticks

Optional
* yellow paper or cellophane

Bible Verse

You are the light of the world. A city on a hill cannot be hidden. Neither do people light a lamp and put it under a bowl. Instead they put it on its stand, and it gives light to everyone in the house. In the same way, let your light shine before men, that they may see your good deeds and praise your Father in heaven (**Matthew 5:14-16**).

Go For It!

1. Photocopy p. 83 onto copier paper.

2. Cut out the figure. Be sure *not* to cut the circle apart from the rest of the figure.

3. Cut out the triangle in the circular roof. Overlap the edges slightly and glue the overlaps to make the roof slightly pointed.

4. Fold each of the panels of the lighthouse on the dotted lines. Place one end section under the opposite end section and glue it in place. Talk with kids about how they can let their light shine as a witness to others.

5. If you wish, tuck a strip of yellow paper or cellophane inside the top of the lighthouse to create a glow.

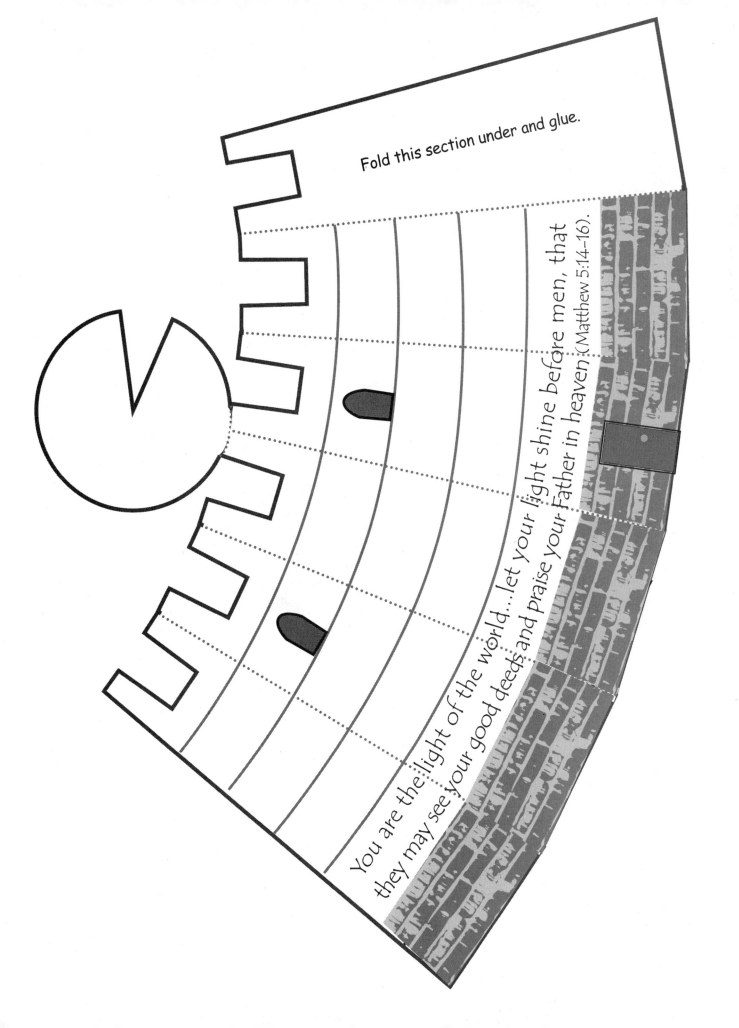

Fold this section under and glue.

You are the light of the world...let your light shine before men, that they may see your good deeds and praise your Father in heaven (Matthew 5:14–16).

The Lord's Prayer My Prayer

Get List

* photocopies of p. 85
* scissors
* colored pencils
* gold and silver markers

Optional:

* tracing paper

Who better to teach your kids to pray than Jesus himself? In this glowing folded card, kids can personalize the prayer Jesus taught his disciples.

Bible Verse

"This, then, is how you should pray: 'Our Father in heaven, hallowed be your name'" **(Matthew 6:9)**.

Go For It!

1. Photocopy p. 85 onto copier paper.

2. Cut out the figure. Have kids fill in their names to personalize the prayer.

3. Decorate the pattern on the circular frame. Let kids add their own personal decorations to the backs of the circles.

4. Show kids how to lap each semi-circle over the next to close the "prayer box." Encourage them to tell you when they'll pray the prayer that Jesus taught.

5. If you wish, trace the figure onto tracing paper. Make a translucent envelope for the prayer—it will be beautiful!

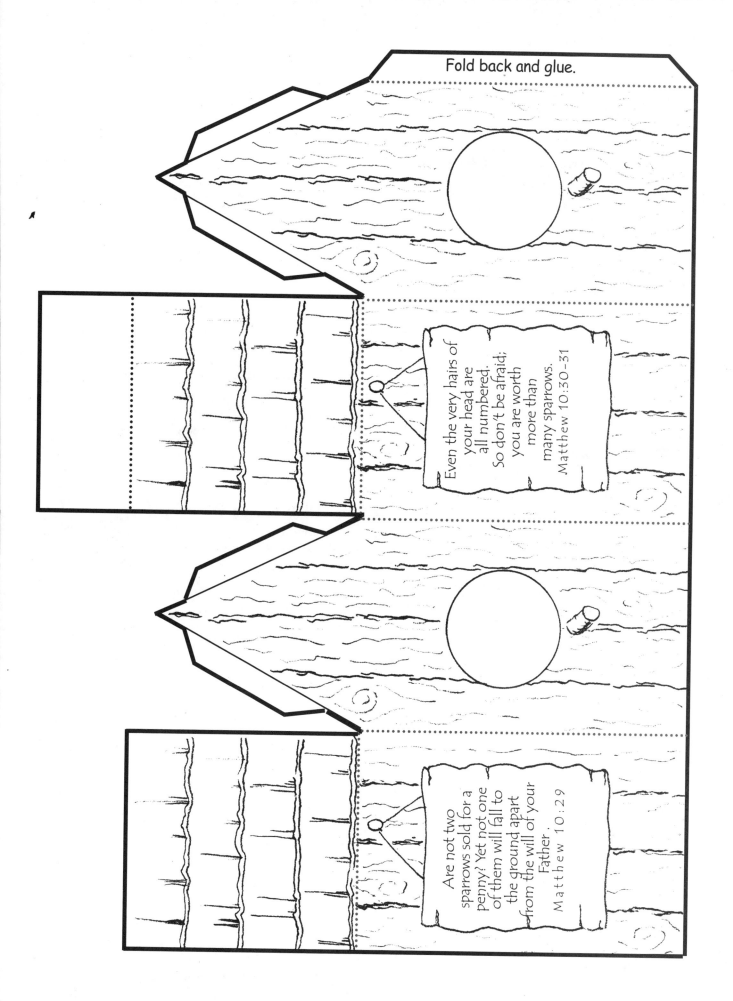

The Great Commission

This simple card recalls two very important messages from Jesus that kids need to remember: "Go" and "I am with you."

Get List

* photocopies of p. 89
* scissors
* glue sticks
* markers

Optional:
* glitter glue
* hair dryer

Bible Verse

Then Jesus came to them and said, "All authority in heaven and on earth has been given to me. Therefore go and make disciples of all nations, baptizing them in the name of the Father and of the Son and of the Holy Spirit, and teaching them to obey everything I have commanded you. And surely I am with you always, to the very end of the age" **(Matthew 28:18-20)**.

Go For It!

1. Photocopy p. 89 onto bright colored paper.

2. Cut out the card and the "GO" circle.

3. Fold the card in half the long way so the pictures show. Then fold the top middle section back and forth on the dotted lines.

4. Unfold the card, then fold it in half the other way. Glue the top edges together on the blank sides. Make sure not to glue the center section.

5. Fold the card in half. Press the center section forward as you fold so that it folds into the card.

6. Open the card. Glue the "GO" circle to the place indicated on the middle section. (Get the placement just right so the circle "hides" when the card is closed.)

7. Decorate the "GO" circle with glitter glue and markers. Have a helper use a blow dryer to dry the glitter glue. As kids write their names on the back of the card, talk about what it means to obey this command and how Jesus is with us.

GO

Glue edge of circle here.

N
E
W
S
O

and make disciples of all nations, baptizing them in the name of the Father and of the Son and of the Holy Spirit, and teaching them to obey everything I have commanded you.

Then Jesus came to them and said, "All authority in heaven and on earth has been given to me. Therefore...

And surely I am with you always, to the very end of the age" (Matthew 28:18-20).

God So Loved

It's a celebration! Kids know what it's like to receive a gift given in love. This vibrant pop-up celebrates God's gift of Jesus, and what that gift means to everyone who receives it.

Get List

* photocopies of p. 91
* scissors
* markers, colored pencils
* glue sticks

Optional
* glitter glue
* hair dryer

Bible Verse

For God so loved the world that he gave his one and only Son, that whoever believes in him shall not perish but have eternal life **(John 3:16)**.

Go For It!

1. Photocopy p. 91 onto copier paper.

2. Cut out the card and the "JESUS" strip. Fold the card in half the long way and glue the blank sides together. Then fold it in half the other way so the Bible Verse shows on the outside of the card.

3. Accordion fold the "JESUS" strip on the dotted lines and glue the end tabs to the spaces indicated on the card.

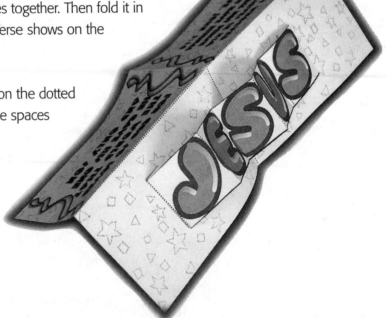

4. Add glitter glue highlights to the card as you talk about what it means to trust in Jesus. Have a helper use a dryer to dry the glitter glue.

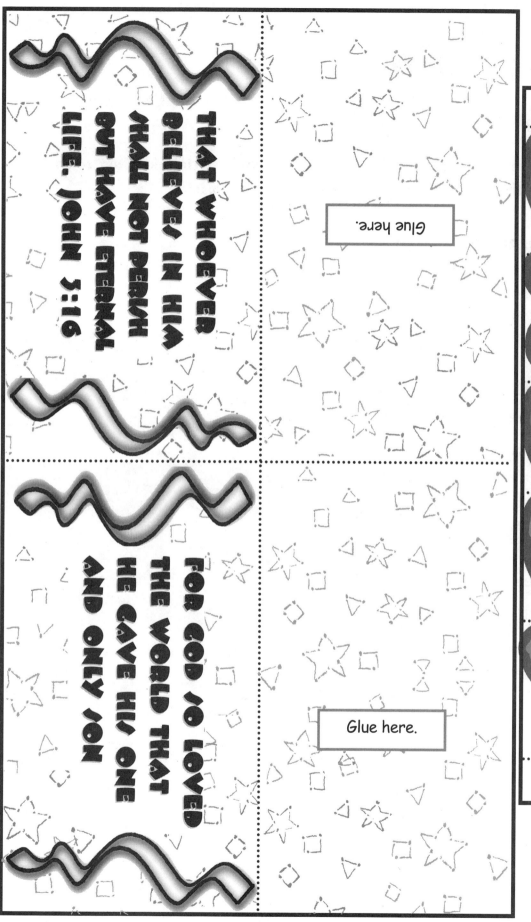

THAT WHOEVER BELIEVES IN HIM SHALL NOT PERISH BUT HAVE ETERNAL LIFE. JOHN 3:16

FOR GOD SO LOVED THE WORLD THAT HE GAVE HIS ONE AND ONLY SON

Glue here.

Glue here.

JESUS

Jesus Said, "I Am..."

Get List

* photocopies of p. 93
* scissors
* glue sticks
* colored pencils

This project unfolds to reveal Jesus' "I Am" statements. Help kids get to know who Jesus is through the statements he made about himself.

Bible Verses

Then Jesus declared, "I am the bread of life" **(John 6:35)**.

"I am the light of the world" **(John 9:5)**.

"I am the good shepherd" **(John 10:14)**.

Jesus said to her, "I am the resurrection and the life. He who believes in me will live" **(John 11:25)**.

Go For It!

1. Photocopy p. 93 onto copier paper.

2. Cut around the figure, then cut it apart on the heavy line.

3. Turn the pieces so the blank side faces you. Place the larger piece on top of the smaller one. Glue the centers together.

4. Fold the "resurrection and the life" page forward and glue it to the blank center piece. The fold the "good shepherd" page forward.

5. Fold the "bread of life" page forward, then the "light of the world" page. As you review the "I am" statements of Jesus, challenge kids to tell you how each statement helps them know Jesus better.

He Is Risen!

Get List

* photocopies of p. 95
* scissors
* pencils
* glue sticks
* cotton swabs

A pure, white lily symbolizes the miracle of Easter when Jesus conquered death. This stunningly realistic craft celebrates the joy of the resurrection.

Bible Verse

The men said to them, "Why do you look for the living among the dead? He is not here; he has risen!" **(Luke 24:5-6)**.

Go For It!

1. Photocopy p. 95 onto copier paper.

2. Give each child three cotton swabs. Use a yellow marker to tint one end of each swab.

3. Cut out the base with the leaves as well as the four lily petals.

4. Fold the dotted lines back on the base piece. Glue the two ends together as shown. You may wish the kids to decorate the base piece before folding it.

5. Fold each of the four lily petals in half the long way so the dotted lines show. Fold the diagonal lines back and forth, then flatten again. Glue two petals together at the bottom as indicated. Do the same with the other two petals.

6. Sandwich three cotton swabs between the two halves of the lily. Let the bottoms of the cotton swabs protrude slightly to form a stem. Glue the bottom of the lily together. Pull the petals outward and roll the tips around a pencil.

7. Place the lily in the base. Talk about how the white lily represents the purity of Jesus' life. Explain that as the perfect sacrifice for the sins of the world, Jesus death and resurrection opened the way to God.

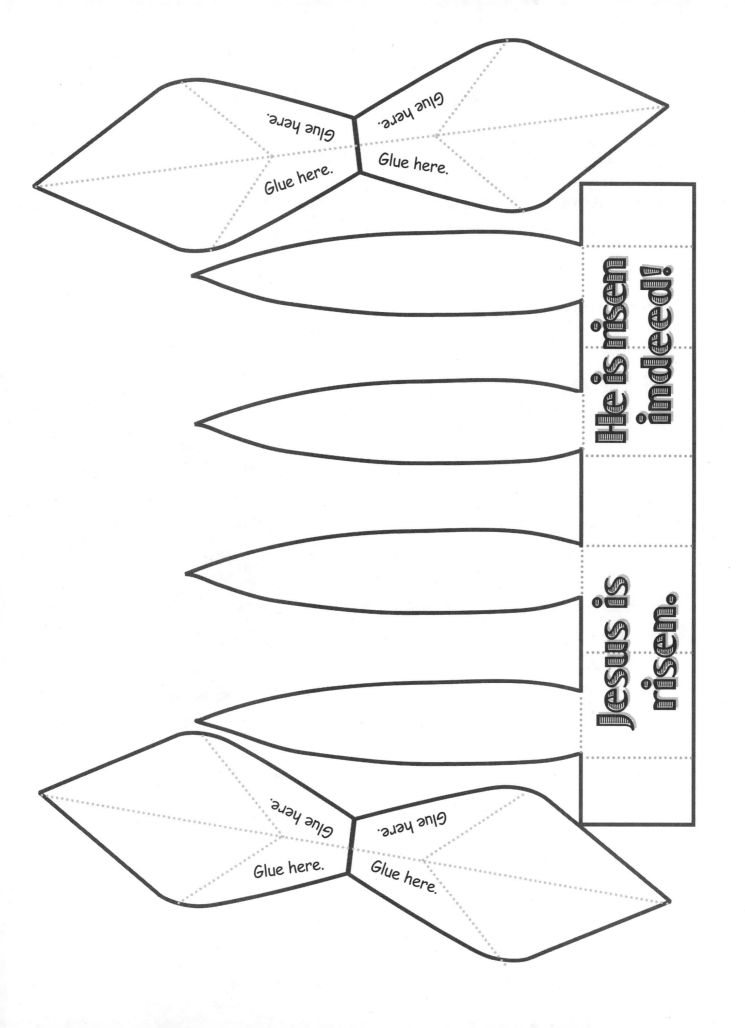

A New You Flutterby

Get List

* photocopies of p. 97
* scissors
* colored pencils

Optional
* glitter glue
* hair dryer

Watch this "flutterby" flit and float in celebration of the new creation each of us becomes when Jesus Christ transforms our lives.

Bible Verse

If anyone is in Christ, he is a new creation; the old has gone, the new has come! **(2 Corinthians 5:17)**.

Go For It!

1. Photocopy p. 97 onto neon-colored paper.

2. Cut out the butterfly.

3. Make a mountain fold on the center dotted line. Make valley folds on the next lines to create wings.

4. Decorate the wings with colored pencils and/or glitter glue. Have a helper dry the glitter glue with a dryer.

5. Toss the butterfly upward like a paper airplane and watch it flit and float to the ground. Talk about what it's like to be a new creation in Christ and how wonderful it is to "fly away" from bad habits and attitudes.

The Fruit of the Spirit

With the power of the Holy Spirit in our lives, we spill over with good fruit! This simple fruit of the spirit basket can spill over with fruit-flavored treats to share.

Bible Verse

But the fruit of the Spirit is love, joy, peace, patience, kindness, goodness, faithfulness, gentleness and self-control **(Galatians 5:22-23)**.

Go For It!

1. Photocopy p. 99 onto brightly colored paper.

2. Cut out and decorate the basket. Cut the side slits on the solid lines.

3. Fold all the dotted lines in. Fold the sides toward the middle. Glue the two smaller sides of the basket together. Then glue the larger side on top of the two smaller sides.

4. Punch holes through the dots in the top of the basket. Fill the basket with treats, then tie ribbon through the holes. Talk about allowing the Holy Spirit to work in us so our lives spill over with good fruit.

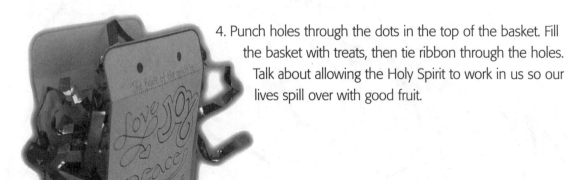

The fruit of the spirit is

Love JOY

peace

PATIENCE

*Kindness

Fold in
and glue.

Fold in
and glue.

Fold in
and glue.

Fold in
and glue.

SELF control

Faithfulness

Gentleness

Goodness

Grin and Bear It

We all need a little help from a friend. This charming bear card will give a little encouragement boost to anyone who receives it.

Get List

* photocopies of p. 101
* scissors
* glue sticks
* colored pencils, markers

Optional:

* glitter glue
* hair dryer

Bible Verse

Bear one another's burdens and so fulfill the law of Christ **(Galatians 6:2, KJV)**.

Go For It!

1. Photocopy p. 101 onto copier paper.

2. Fold the card in half the long way so the pictures show. Cut the banner on the dark lines between the dots. Unfold.

3. Fold the card in half the other way so the pictures show. Close the card, pushing the banner forward so it pops out when the card is opened. Lightly glue the inside bottom corners and sides so the "front" of the card and the "inside" of the card don't come apart.

4. Decorate the card. If kids use glitter glue, have a helper dry it with a hair dryer.

5. Talk about who would get a lift from receiving a card of encouragement, and how kids can follow up to show their support.

I know it's hard to
grin and bear it...

Bear one another's
burdens and so
fulfill the law
of Christ
(Galatians 6:2, KJV).

So remember...

I'm your biggest fan!

Put on Love

There's a moose on the loose, and he's got some great "wearables" from Colossians 3. This stand-up figure will remind kids how to dress every day!

Get List

* photocopies of p. 103
* scissors
* colored pencils, markers

Bible Verse

Therefore, as God's chosen people, holy and dearly loved, clothe yourselves with compassion, kindness, humility, gentleness and patience. Bear with each other and forgive whatever grievances you may have against one another. Forgive as the Lord forgave you. And over all these virtues put on love, which binds them all together in perfect unity **(Colossians 3:12-14)**.

Go For It!

1. Photocopy p. 103 onto sturdy paper.

2. Cut out and decorate the moose figure. Fold the tabs back on the dotted lines to form a stand.

3. Cut the slits on the base. Hook them together to make Mr. Moose stand up.

4. Talk about each of the characteristics God wants us to put on. Which are easy to "wear"? Which are more challenging? How can God help us "be dressed" this way?

Therefore, as God's chosen people, holy and dearly loved, clothe yourselves with compassion, kindness, humility, gentleness and patience. Bear with each other and forgive whatever grievances

you may have against one another. Forgive as the Lord forgave you. And over all these virtues put on love, which binds them all together in perfect unity. Colossians 3:12-14

You've Got Mail

This miniature mailbox can deliver all kind of little messages of hope from your kids to parents, church workers or whoever needs a lift.

Get List

* photocopies of p. 105
* scissors
* glue sticks
* colored pencils, markers

Optional
* wrapped candies

Bible Verse

Therefore encourage one another and build each other up, just as in fact you are doing **(1 Thessalonians 5:11)**.

Go For It!

1. Photocopy p. 105 onto copier paper.

2. Cut out and decorate the two pieces. Address the mailbox and decorate the mailbox and the doors.

3. Make mountain folds on the dotted lines on the long strip with the Bible Verse. Overlap the ends of the strip and glue in place. This makes the main mailbox form.

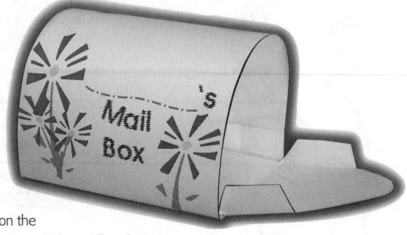

4. Mountain fold the two curved ends of the plain base to form the doors of the mailbox. Fold the four tabs in on the dotted lines. Slip the plain strip through the mailbox form. Glue the middle section down. Fold the two doors up, pushing the tabs inside the mailbox to hold the doors closed.

5. Fill the mailbox with treats. Talk about the power of encouragement and let kids plan how they'll deliver their mailboxes.

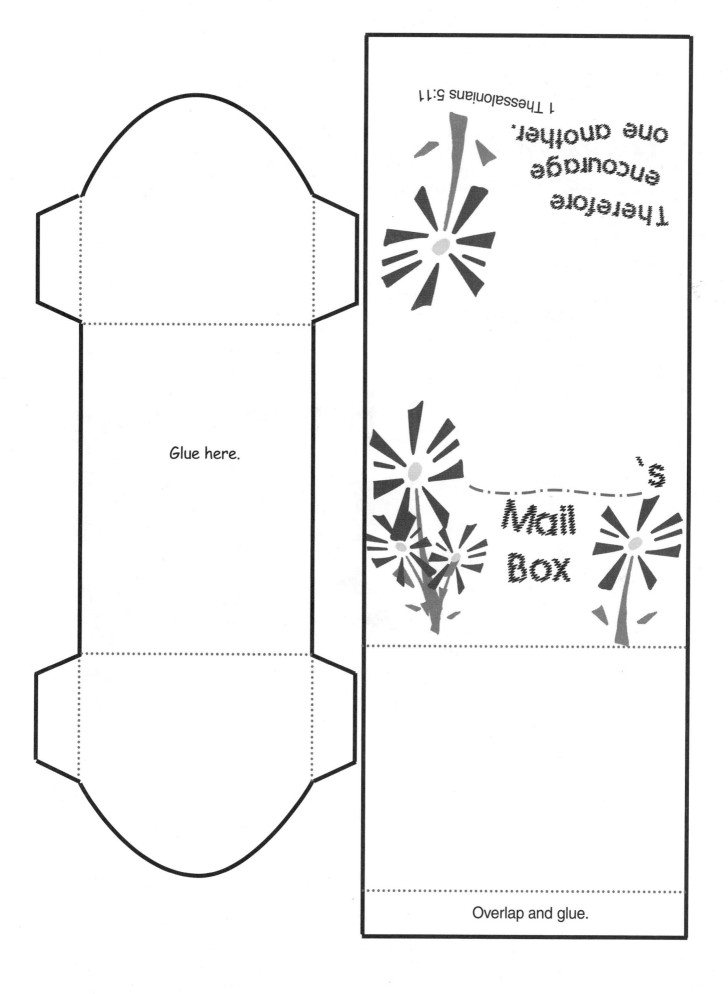

Glue here.

Therefore encourage
one another.

1 Thessalonians 5:11

__'s

Mail
Box

Overlap and glue.

Stairway to Happiness

Get List

* photocopies of p. 107
* scissors
* construction paper
* glue sticks
* colored pencils, markers

Kids will have a hard time missing these steps to happiness and a godly life!

Bible Verse

Be joyful always; pray continually; give thanks in all circumstances, for this is God's will for you in Christ Jesus **(1 Thessalonians 5:16-18)**.

Go For It!

1. Photocopy p. 107 on copier paper.

2. Fold the pattern in half on the middle dotted line so that the words show. Cut the dark lines between the dots. Unfold, then decorate the letters.

3. Valley fold on the middle dotted line, then on the two other dotted lines. Mountain fold on the two dashed lines. Pull the steps forward.

4. Fold a sheet of construction paper in half. Glue it behind the pattern to form a backing sheet. Encourage kids to take these steps every day!

Be

always

continually

in all circumstances, for this is
God's will for you in
Christ Jesus.
1 Thessalonians 5:16–18

Love One Another

This hidden heart full of love makes a wonderful card for Valentine's Day or anytime!

Get List

* photocopies of p. 109
* scissors
* glue sticks
* craft knife

Optional
* shiny wrapping paper
* glitter glue or stickers
* hair dryer
* shiny bag stuffing or small treats

Bible Verse

Dear friends, let us love one another, for love comes from God. Everyone who loves has been born of God and knows God (**1 John 4:7**).

Go For It!

1. Photocopy p. 109 onto pink or red paper.

2. Cut out the background and the two hearts.

3. Fold the tabs on the hearts back. Glue each tab to the opposite heart to form a pocket. Be sure to keep the points free of glue.

4. Have older kids or helpers open the slit in the background piece. Slide the point of the heart pocket through the slit. Fold one point forward and the other back on the dotted lines. Glue these points to the back of the card.

5. Add stickers or dots of glitter glue to the heart pocket and card. Let a helper dry the glitter glue with a hair dryer. If you wish, fill the heart pockets with small treats or shiny bag stuffing. Fold the card in half so the Bible Verse and heart pocket are inside the card.

6. Let kids plan who will receive their cards, then write personal messages of appreciation on the front and back. Or, back the card with shiny wrapping paper.

(1 John 4:7)

Everyone who
loves has been
born of God and
knows God

_____

Dear friends,
let us love one
another, for
love comes
from God.

Bonus Patterns

Use these patterns as name tags or notes. The notes will fit in the envelope on p. 111. Use the letter/envelope on P. 112 for personal notes or flyers. Fold it with the pattern inside or out.

c p a a p p e e r r s

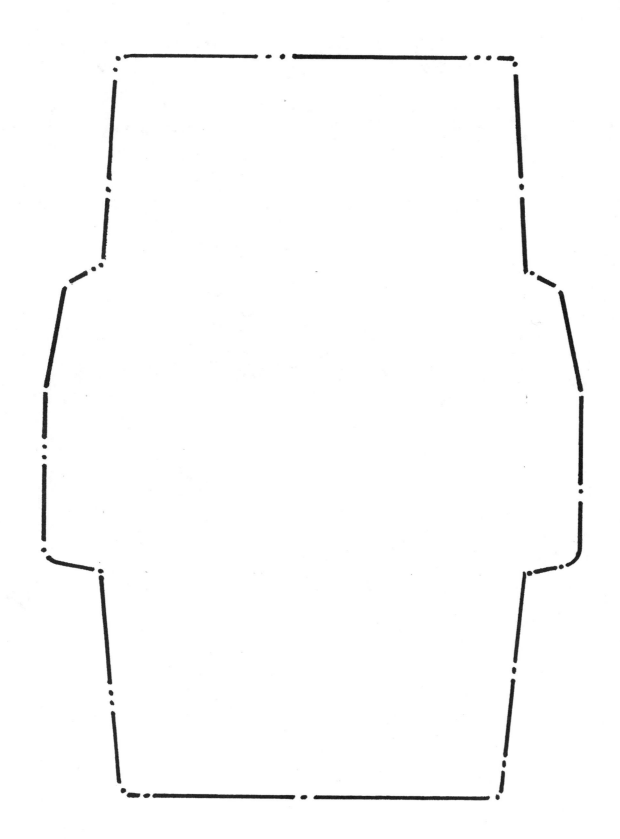

WHAT'S UP